Contents

Foreword

Everybody likes to create something beautiful, something that moves other people to say, 'How lovely! Did you make it yourself?' Such pieces of work are very welcome as presents – people will be aware of the time and trouble you have taken as well as appreciating the quilts themselves.

The materials I like to experiment with are paper and fabric. From the iris paper-folding technique for making greetings cards that I developed in the year 2000, it was a logical step to my other favourite occupation: quilting. I converted a number of my paper models into fabric designs, and that is how I made the iris quilts in this book. All the designs can be stitched by hand and/or using a sewing machine, depending on your preference. The quilts are made using the 'paper-piecing method': you sew the strips of fabric on to a thin backing, following the numbers on the pattern. The strips of fabric are then trimmed in a tapering shape, which gives the pattern a swirling motion. This has a striking effect and becomes even more exciting when different patterns, such as triangles and squares, are combined. All this sounds complicated, but it isn't really. Just follow the instructions carefully and you will be sure to get it right.

What makes your iris quilts your own is your personal choice of colours. You can copy the colour templates and fill them in a number of times until you find the most attractive combination. Then choose your pieces of fabric, cut them into strips and put your iris quilt together. Making a little quilt like this is a wonderful pastime.

Just as the coloured iris of the eye surrounds the pupil, so the coloured strips of fabric surround the heart of every iris quilt. Wishing you lots of inspiration and creative pleasure,

Maruscha

Techniques

The iris quilt is a special form of log cabin quilt: an idea comes to life by sewing various fabric patches on to a thin backing following a pattern. The distinctive feature of iris quilts is the spiralling movement around the centre, the 'heart', created using tapering strips placed next to each other to resemble the iris in the lens of a camera. One by one, the numbered sections on the backing material are covered by fabric strips, with the colours arranged in a regular sequence and firmly sewn on. A four-sided 'heart' usually involves fabric in four different colours, while a triangular one needs at least three colours for the rotation to be visible. Choose fabrics with small motifs and plain solid colours that make a pleasant combination and contrast – a Jelly Roll bundle of 6 × 110cm (2½ × 43in) pieces of coordinating fabric is perfect for this. Always use enough material to cover each section of the pattern completely. In my instructions, I assume a seam allowance of between 6mm (¼in) and 1cm (⅜in) per strip, depending on the thickness and pile of the material and the way it has been processed. By trimming each strip to shape once you have sewn it in place, you will work quickly and smoothly.

Colours

The choice of coloured fabric is very important to the whole creation and so every pattern is shown completed here in colour. The templates are like ready-made quilts. Each pattern is a mirror image of the final quilt. It would be a good idea to copy out your own selection of a number of the colour templates. Treat yourself to a nice box of coloured pencils, make a fresh pot of tea, choose a cosy corner and spend some quiet time trying out colour schemes based on your fabrics. It is well worth the trouble, as it can prevent disappointing results from your needlework. Besides, it is fun.

Paper piecing

This is a method of quilting in which your fabric pieces are stitched to a lightweight foundation on which the pattern has been marked. It is especially effective with small or complex designs because it ensures accuracy. For the patterns in this book, a lightweight white sew-in interfacing such as Vilene L11 is used as the foundation, as it is supple and well adapted to sewing. Nappy lining and special thin paper are alternatives to Vilene L11. With good transparent material, the sequenced strips can be pinned and sewn on directly from the numbered side of the pattern. This is quicker because the work does not have to be turned over so often.

Transferring the design

To transfer your design to the interfacing, first tape a copy of your chosen pattern firmly on to your cutting mat and then tape the interfacing over it. With a sharp pencil or pen, carefully and accurately trace the entire pattern, including the numbers. This is the sewing side. The fabrics will be placed one by one on the other side and stitched in place. The centre (the 'heart') will be covered first, and then the strips will be stitched on in number order so that the interfacing is continually moved round in a circle. The quilt will be the mirror image of the drawn pattern.

Fabrics

All the quilts are made from 100% cotton fabric, except for the wadding (batting) and a number of the quilt hearts. Sometimes these hearts are made from a piece of holographic paper or often from glossy stretch fabric for special effect. The measurements given in the requirement lists are height × width. The height indicates the depth of the fabric strips, while the width is divided into smaller quantities, strip by strip. If you are required to cut a piece of yellow fabric measuring 20 × 12cm (8 × 4¾in) into 3cm (1¼in) strips, this means you must cut out four strips 20cm (8in) deep. Alternatively you can cut strips of fabric to size as you need them. Jelly Roll fabric must always be cut lengthways. Since no strip will be wider than 6cm (2½in), this material is ideal for iris quilts.

Thread

When sewing the strips on to the interfacing and when assembling the quilt, use a thread in a matching colour so that the stitching will be as invisible as possible. No colours are specified in my instructions. In a few of quilts, the colour of the thread is just noticeable enough to add something to the pattern, as on the perfume-bottle quilt on page 64, in which case the colours are specified in the text.

Meandering background stitching

I stitch the background areas of the quilted layers in a meandering line that flows naturally in the same way that a river winds through the landscape (see the Heart to Heart quilt on page 11). This is free-motion stitching which requires that you lower the feed dogs on your machine and work with an embroidery foot or darning-foot – see the instruction manual that came with your sewing machine for information on setting it up for free-motion stitching. Work at a slow, steady pace, using both hands to move the fabric in a continual wave motion under the needle, to the left, then away from you, then right, then back towards you. Keep this up until you have filled the whole background area. In order to get a nice flowing stitch,

I recommend that you first try a practice fabric sample made up of top, wadding and backing material. The refined effect you can see in the Heart to Heart quilt is due to the use of the same colour thread as the backing material.

Mitred borders

If you wish to add a mitred border, as shown on Light Your Way, page 88, first stitch the top and side borders of your piece up to where they meet at the corners, making sure that at least the width of the border plus that of the seam project beyond each corner. Fold the outer end of the side border under at an angle of 45° to the side as an extension of the upper border. Iron the fold flat, place what is left over from the side border on the top border and sew the borders together over the right-angled fold. Trim the seam allowance short and unfold it.

Bias binding

The binding for the quilts in this book is produced with an 18mm (¾in) bias-binding maker. First cut regular or tapering fabric strips to the width specified in the instructions. Insert a strip into the wide end of the machine and guide it further with a pin until the folded edge can be clearly seen at the other end. It is easier if you pin the edge to your ironing board and press the folds with a warm iron before putting them through the bias-binding maker.

Assembly and hanging

Directions for putting the quilts together are given separately for each piece. How you hang your quilt is a matter of personal preference, but the usual preferred method is to hang it from a wooden pole or dowel threaded through a sleeve on the back of the quilt because this distributes the weight of the quilt evenly. This is the method used to hang Spring Flowers (page 36). Alternatively you can use a metal hanger, as was used for The Perfect Pear (page 84). With smaller quilts, you can be more inventive – loops are sufficient to hang the Colour and Scent (page 64) and heart-shaped paperclips secure A Rose for all Seasons (page 80).

Where to start

It is important to begin by following the step-by-step instructions for the heart quilt (see pages 9–10). The clear photographs and accompanying text will teach you the unique iris-quilting method stage by stage. The basis of this technique is that all the numbered sections of the pattern are covered, from the centre outwards and in a circular order, with fabric strips in different colours. Once you have mastered this technique, you will have absolutely no difficulty in making the other quilts.

Step-by-step working method

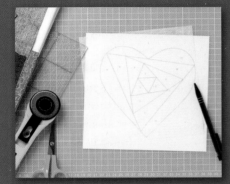

1 Using a pencil, trace the pattern with numbered sections on to lightweight white sew-in interfacing. This is heart B, page 12.

2 Turn the interfacing over and pin your small square of glossy fabric right side up over the 'heart' at the centre.

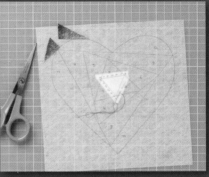

3 Turn the interfacing back over and tack just outside the pattern lines. Trim the fabric to shape, allowing a small allowance all round.

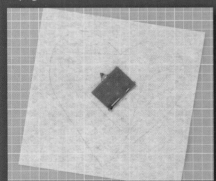

4 On the fabric side, place your first strip of fabric right side down on the 'heart' fabric at section 1. (The strip shown is plain red on the wrong side and patterned with white on the right side.)

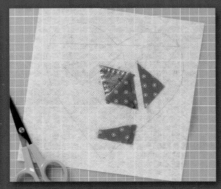

5 Turn the interfacing over again and sew along the stitching line. Turn over again, open out the strip, trim off the excess fabric (remembering to leave seam allowances) and pin it in place.

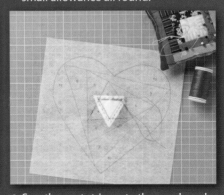

6 Sew the next strip on to the numbered side along the stitching line of section 2. In this example the strip being attached is dark red (see step 7, overleaf).

Step-by-step working method continued

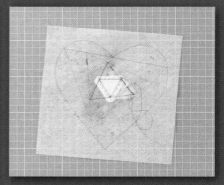

7 Turn the interfacing over again, open out the strip (dark red), trim off the excess fabric and pin it in place.

8 Pin on the next strip as before. This is the last strip of the first round and is shown here in pink.

9 Turn the interfacing over and sew along the stitching line. Repeat the same process for the second round, working in number order.

10 The second round is complete. Press your work as you go for a neat result.

Once the quilt layers have been assembled, I like to work meandering lines of free-motion machine stitching over plain background areas (see page 7).

Here is the finished heart with a little meandering on the white background fabric.

Heart to Heart

This romantic quilt features two hearts in mirror image, gently touching (see the photograph on page 7). It is a good place to begin because the design is very straightforward and you can follow the step-by-step instruction on pages 9–10.

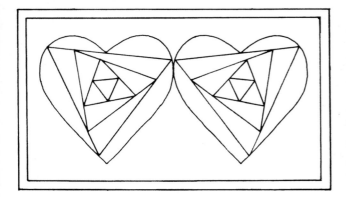

Heart template

Quilt size: 29 × 43cm (11½ × 17in)
Pattern size: 15 × 15cm (6 × 6in)

Method

1 Cut out three strips 4.5cm (1¾in) wide from the red, the dark red and the pink fabrics. Trace heart pattern A (for the right-hand heart) from page 12, including the numbers, on to the interfacing. Turn the interfacing over and pin the gold glossy fabric over the 'heart', right side up. Turn the interfacing back to the side with the numbers on and tack the glossy fabric to the interfacing, just outside the stitching line. Turn your work over again and cut the fabric into the triangular shape of the heart, leaving a small seam allowance all round.

2 Pin 5 × 4.5cm (2 × 1¾in) of red fabric right side down over the heart by the stitching line of section 1, keeping the upper edge level with the edge of the glossy fabric. Turn the interfacing over to the side bearing the numbers and sew the fabrics together along the stitching line of section 1. Turn your work over again and trim the seam allowance short. Open out the red strip, spread it over section 1 and press it flat. Pin the strip on to the next stitching line.

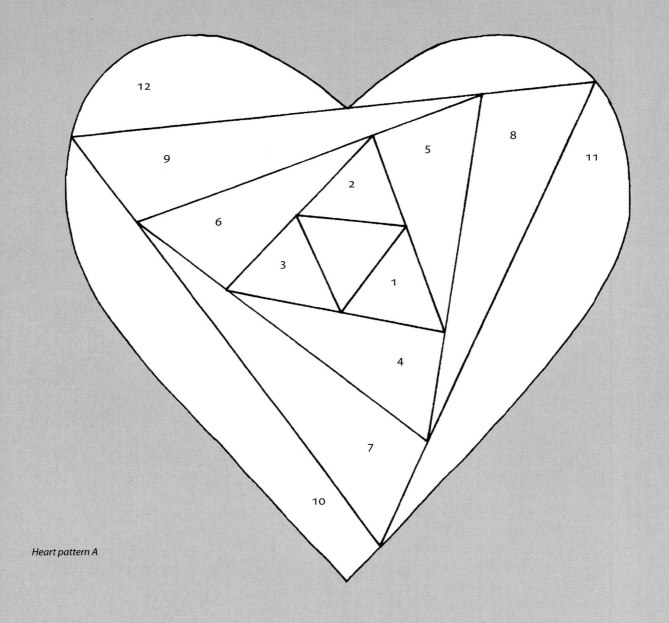

Heart pattern A

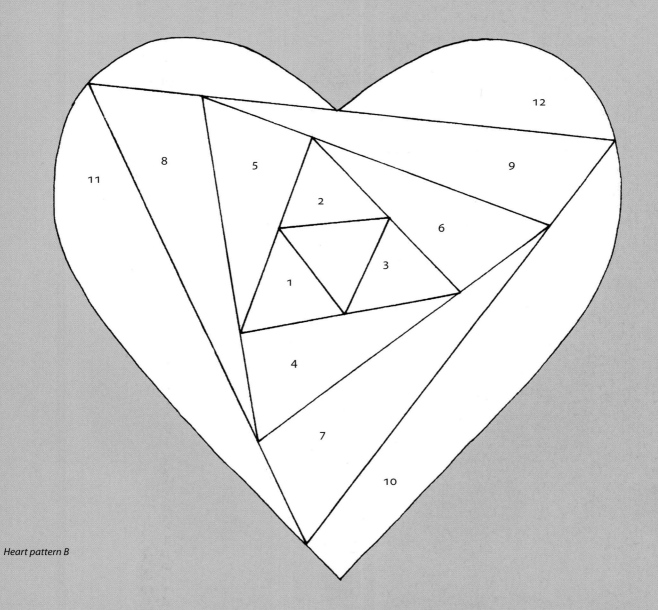

Heart pattern B

3 Pin 5 × 4.5cm (2 × 1¾in) of dark red fabric right side down over the heart by the stitching line of section 2, keeping the upper edge level with the edge of the glossy fabric. Turn the interfacing over and sew the fabrics together along the stitching line of section 2. Turn your work over again and trim the seam allowance short. Open out the dark red strip, spread it over section 2 and press it flat. Pin the strip on to the next stitching line.

4 Pin 5 × 4.5cm (2 × 1¾in) of pink fabric right side down over the heart by the stitching line of section 3, keeping the upper edge level with the edge of the glossy fabric. Turn the interfacing over and sew the fabrics together along the stitching line of section 3. Turn your work over again and trim the seam allowance short. Open out the pink strip, spread it over section 3 and press it flat. Pin the strip on to the next stitching line.

5 The first round is now finished. Leaving a seam allowance, snip off any bits that are sticking out, so that you can see which way the strips will go in the next round.

What to do next

1 Repeat the procedure described above from step 2 onwards with increasingly long strips in order to fill sections 4, 5, 6, etc. You will find the right measurements for the fabric by measuring on the pattern and adding a generous seam allowance. In the second round, you will use red fabric for section 4, then dark red fabric for section 5, then pink fabric for section 6, and so on. Keep alternating the three colours, but always in the same order.

2 For the second heart, trace pattern B (page 13), including the numbers, on to interfacing. The rotation around this heart is anticlockwise, but the method is the same as described above. Complete the second heart.

Putting it all together

1 Using small stitches, tack around the heart, slightly outside the stitching line. Cut out each heart with a 6mm (¼in) seam allowance all round. Carefully draw the tacking thread tight, gathering the seam allowance so that the raw edges fold to the back.

2 Using red, dark red and pink thread and a small needle, attach the hearts to the white-flowered background fabric with tiny stitches round the edges, each part attached with thread of its own colour. Cut the red fabric for the narrow border into four 2.5 × 36cm (1 × 14¼in) strips and attach one to each side and then one to the top and then the bottom edge. Cut the fabric for the wide white-flowered borders into four equal strips and attach them, first to the sides, then to the top and bottom edges.

Finishing off

Make a quilt sandwich with the wadding between the top quilt and backing, right sides out, and tack the layers. Meander over the white fabric around the hearts using your sewing machine, with white thread on the spool and bobbin for a refined effect (see Techniques). Hand quilt the outer border 1cm (⅜in) and 1.5cm (⅝in) outside the red edging (see the photograph on page 7). Neatly trim the edges of the quilt. Put the four binding strips through the bias-binding maker and bind the edges of the quilt.

Lullaby for a Hedgehog

This sweet little hedgehog makes a lovely wall decoration for a child's bedroom. His spines and eye are embroidered and the small leaves are cut from fabric and then loosely attached to add to the three-dimensional element.

Quilt size: 24 × 30cm (9½ × 12in)
Pattern size: 8 × 14.5cm (3¼ × 5¾in)

Method

1 Cut strips 3.5cm (1⅜in) wide for the hedgehog: three each from the patterned brown and warm brown fabrics and four from the patterned pale yellow fabric. Cut out a strip 7cm (2¾in) wide from the yellow fabric and four strips 3.5cm (1⅜in) wide from the remaining 9 × 14cm (3½ × 5½in) of this fabric.

2 Trace the hedgehog pattern from page 18, including the numbers, on to interfacing. Turn the interfacing over and pin the red glossy fabric over the 'heart', right side up. Turn your work over again and tack the fabric to the interfacing, just outside the stitching lines. Turn your work over yet again and trim the glossy fabric into the shape of the heart, leaving a small seam allowance.

3 The first section is rather fiddly to cover because of its shape. Cut a 4cm (1½in) piece of warm brown fabric. The easiest attachment method is to fold a point to the shape of the section where it joins the heart and then hand stitch it in place from the right side. All the other pieces are attached in the usual way. Press the strip flat and pin it on to the next stitching line.

4 Cut 3.5cm (1⅜in) from a pale yellow strip and pin it right side down over the heart by the stitching line of section 2,

For the hedgehog
• 9 × 21cm (3½ × 8¼in) of yellow fabric • 10 × 10.5cm (4 × 4⅛in) of patterned brown fabric • 8 × 14cm (3¼ × 5½in) of patterned pale yellow fabric
• 10 × 10.5cm (4 × 4⅛in) of warm brown fabric
• 3 × 3.5cm (1¼ × 1⅜in) of red glossy fabric • Scrap of black fabric for the nose

For the rest
• 12cm (4¾in) square of fabric with a small leaf motif for the appliquéd leaves (or more if necessary to obtain sufficient leaves) • 12cm (4¾in) square of iron-on interfacing • 18 × 25cm (7 × 10in) of off-white fabric for the background • 100 × 5cm (39½ × 2in) of brown leafy fabric for the border and 33 × 14cm (13 × 5½in) for the binding • Dark brown embroidery silk • Dark brown and yellow sewing thread and dark brown and ivory-white quilting thread • 28 × 34cm (11 × 13½in) of wadding (batting) • 28 × 34cm (11 × 13½in) of backing fabric • 12 × 16cm (4¾ × 6¼in) of lightweight white sew-in interfacing, e.g. Vilene L11 • 18mm (¾in) bias-binding maker

keeping the upper edge level with the edge of the glossy fabric. Turn your work over to the side bearing the numbers

and sew the fabrics together along the stitching line of section 2. Turn your work over again and trim the seam allowance short. Open out the light yellow strip, spread it over section 2 and press it flat. Pin the strip on to the next stitching line.

Note: there is no section 3, so leave the patterned brown fabric out of this first round.

5 Cut out 4cm (1½in) from a yellow strip and pin it right side down over the heart by the stitching line of section 4, upper edge level with the edge of the glossy fabric. Turn your work over to the side bearing the numbers and sew the fabrics together along the stitching line of section 4. Trim the seam allowance short. Open out the yellow strip, spread it over section 4 and press it flat. Pin the strip on to the next stitching

line. The first round is now finished. Leaving a small seam allowance, snip off any bits that are sticking out so that you can see which way the strips will go in the next round.

What to do next

The colour sequence of the strips in the second round is warm brown for section 5, light yellow for section 6, then, for the first time, the patterned brown fabric for section 7, and yellow for section 8. Repeat the procedure described above, using increasingly long strips in order to fill sections 9, 10, 11, etc. Cover sections 20a and 20b both together with a wide strip of yellow fabric measuring 9 × 7cm (3½ × 2¾in) and sew them into position through the middle, so that the head of the hedgehog is formed from doubled fabric. Cut a 1.5cm (⅝in)

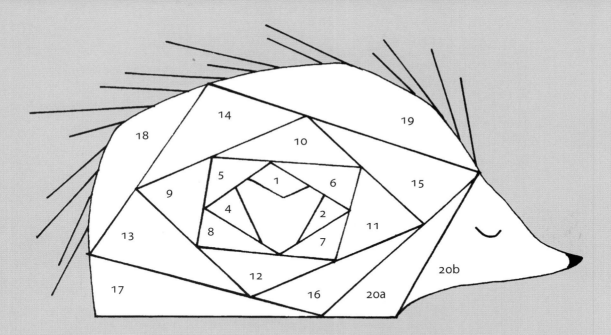

Hedgehog pattern

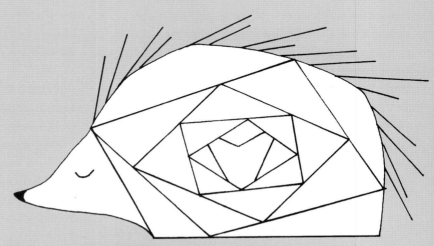

Hedgehog template

Copy and colour in the template with the colours of your fabrics

triangle from the black fabric, roll it up into a point and sew it in place as the hedgehog's nose.

Putting it all together

1 Tack the outer fabric strips to the interfacing with small stitches just beyond the outline. Cut out the hedgehog with a seam allowance of 6mm (¼in) all round. Carefully pull up the tacking thread tight, gathering the seam allowance so that it folds over to the back. Stitch the hedgehog to the off-white background fabric with thread of the same colour as the fabric strips. Add the eye and the spines with small embroidery stitches.

2 Reinforce the fabric for the little leaves with iron-on interfacing. Cut out a number of leaves and sew them on

below the hedgehog's body, also attaching a sprig to one of his spines. Cut the brown leafy fabric to fit the sides and stitch in place. Cut and attach another strip to the top and one to the bottom edge.

Finishing off

Make a quilt sandwich with the wadding between the top quilt and backing, right sides out, and tack the layers. Quilt the layers as desired. In this example, the quilting centres on the hedgehog and includes a border of little moons (from the words of the Dutch lullaby, 'Out there the moon is shining'). Trim the edges neatly to size. Cut the 33 × 14cm (13 × 5½in) rectangle of brown leaf-pattern fabric into strips 3.5cm (1⅜in) wide and run them through the binding maker. Bind the quilt with these.

Dance of the Butterflies

Three blue butterflies flutter back and forth over an off-white background on this light and airy quilt hanging. The same four blue fabrics are used for all the butterflies but in different positions for added variation.

Quilt size: 58 × 27cm (23 × 10¾in)
Pattern size: 17 × 18cm (6¾ × 7in)

Note

The top and bottom butterflies are both made using pattern A, while the central butterfly uses pattern B. The directions are for the upper butterfly, but can be applied to all the butterflies except that the colours are arranged differently. You make the right wing first, then the left wing and finally the body in between.

Method

1 Trace butterfly pattern A from page 22, including the numbers and lettered spaces, on to the interfacing with a pencil. Cover the 'heart' (the kite shape in the centre of the wing) on the reverse side with a generous quantity of the silver glossy fabric, right side up, and pin this in place. Turn the interfacing over and tack the glossy fabric on to the interfacing, just outside the stitching lines. Turn your work over again and cut the fabric to the shape of the heart, leaving a small seam allowance all round.

2 For section 1, pin a strip measuring 6 × 3cm (2½ × 1¼in) of colour 1 (mid-blue floral) right side down over the heart by the stitching line of section 1, keeping the upper edge level with the edge of the glossy heart. Turn your work over to the side bearing the numbers, and sew the strip along the stitching line of section 1. Turn your work over again and trim the seam

For each butterfly
- Fabric 1 (mid-blue floral): 28 × 12cm (11 × 5in) cut into four strips, 3cm (1¼in) wide • Fabric 2 (dark blue): 14 × 12cm (5½ × 5in) cut into four strips, 3cm (1¼in) wide • Fabric 3 (white patterned with blue): 16 × 14cm (6¼ × 5½in) cut into four strips, 3.5cm (1⅜in) wide • Fabric 4 (royal blue): 20 × 14cm (8 × 5½in) cut into three strips, 3.5cm (1⅜in) wide • 8 × 3cm (3¼ × 1¼in) of blue velvet for the body • 7 × 8cm (2¾ × 3¼in) of holographic paper or glossy fabric (blue or silver) for the heart in each wing • 20cm (8in) square of lightweight white sew-in interfacing, e.g. Vilene L11 • 32 × 22cm (12½ × 8¾in) of off-white fabric for filling in

For the rest
- 60 × 18cm (23½ × 7½in) of off-white fabric for the border • 62 × 32cm (24½ × 12½in) of off-white fabric for the backing • 62 × 32cm (24½ × 12½in) of wadding (batting) • Blue embroidery silk for the antennae • Quilting thread in off-white, yellow, orange and burgundy for the 'flower scents' • 2m (2¼yd) of off-white bias binding

allowance short. Open out the strip, spread it over section 1 and press it flat. Pin the strip on to the next stitching line.

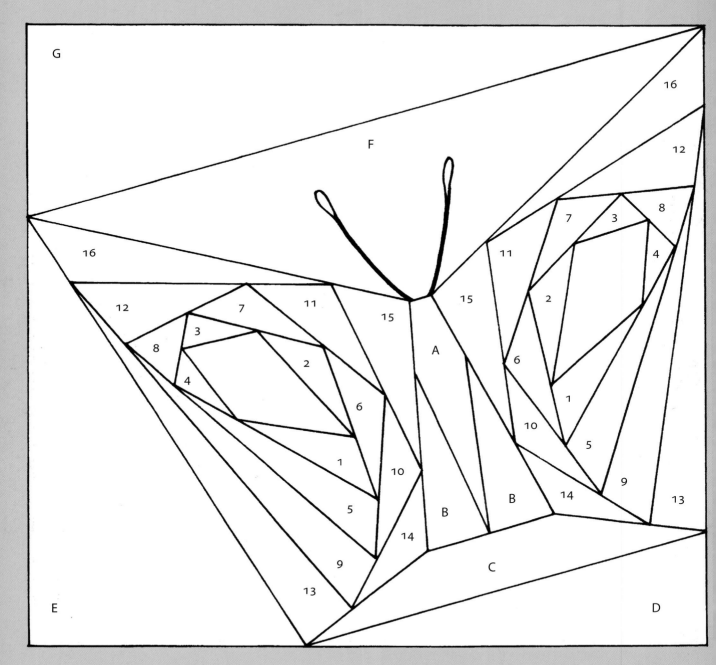

Butterfly pattern A

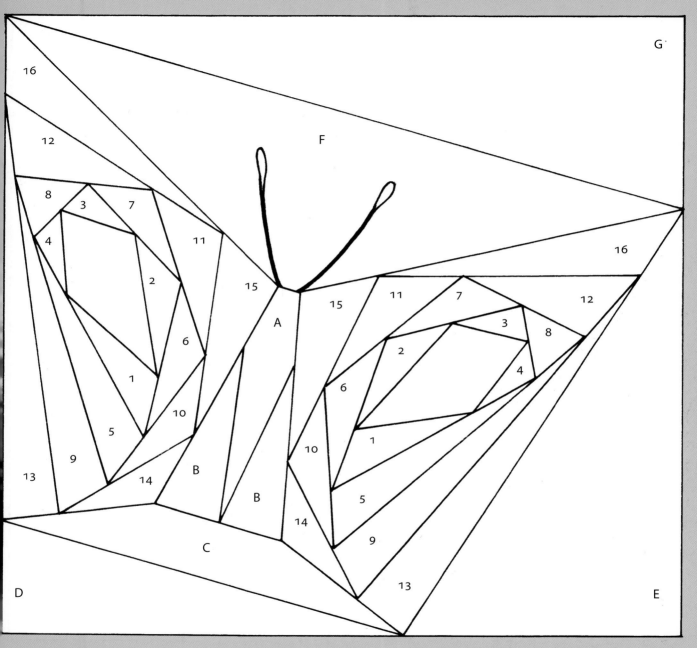

Butterfly pattern B

Butterflies A and B

the strip along the stitching line of section 3. Turn your work over again and trim the seam allowance short. Open out the strip, spread it over section 3 and press it flat. Pin the strip on to the next stitching line.

5   For section 4, pin a strip measuring 4 × 3.5cm (1½ × 1⅜in) of colour 4 (royal blue) right side down over the heart by section 4, keeping the upper edge level with the edge of the glossy heart. Turn your work over and sew the strip along the stitching line of section 4. Turn your work over again and trim the seam allowance short. Open out the blue strip, spread it over section 3 and press it flat. Pin the strip on to the next stitching line. You have completed the first round.

What to do next

Repeat the procedure described above from step 2 onwards, measuring out a generous strip length for each section you are going to cover. Follow the number order and keep alternating colours 1, 2, 3 and 4, always in the same sequence. Fill the other wing with the same sequence of colours as the first wing, but in reverse order: mid-blue floral for sections 1, 5, 9 and 13; dark blue for sections 2, 6, 10 and 14; white patterned with blue for sections 3, 7, 11 and 15, and royal blue for sections 4, 8, 12 and 16. When you have finished both wings, sew the fillers B on to each side of the body A and the whole combination on to section 15 of one wing. Open out body A and filling pieces B, fold the seam allowance to the back and attach it with small overcast stitches to section 15, the edge of the other wing.

3   For section 2, pin a strip measuring 6 × 3cm (2½ × 1¼in) of colour 2 (dark blue) right side down over the heart by section 2, keeping the upper edge level with the edge of the glossy heart. Turn your work over and sew the strip along the stitching line of section 2. Turn your work over again and trim the seam allowance short. Open out the dark blue strip, spread it over section 2 and press it flat. Pin the strip on to the next stitching line.

4   For section 3, pin a strip measuring 4 × 3.5cm (1½ × 1⅜in) of colour 3 (white patterned with blue) right side down over the heart by section 3, keeping the upper edge level with the edge of the glossy heart. Turn your work over and sew

Putting it all together

1 Sew filling pieces C (partly with overcast stitching), D, E, F and G, in that order, to the interfacing. Iron the butterfly on the back. If holographic paper is used for the heart, as in the example, iron this first and then see to the surrounding area.

2 Make the other two butterfly units, using pattern B for the central butterfly, for which the colour sequence on the wings is: 1 royal blue, 2 mid-blue floral, 3 dark blue and 4 white patterned with blue. For the bottom butterfly, the colour sequence is: 1 white patterned with blue, 2 royal blue, 3 mid-blue floral and 4 dark blue. The wing hearts are made from silver and blue glossy fabric and the bodies from blue velvet in different shades.

Finishing off

Place the three butterfly units together. Cut out strips 6cm (2½in) wide from the off-white border fabric and sew them first to the top and bottom edges, then to the side edges. Press the top quilt. Make a quilt sandwich with the wadding between the top quilt and backing, right sides out, and tack the layers. Quilt as you wish. The 'flower scents' are hand quilted using coloured thread and the border is quilted in off-white thread. Embroider the butterflies' antennae using the blue silk. Trim the edges neatly and then bind them.

Up in a Balloon

This clever, colourful quilt will brighten any room and inspire you to dream. It can be even more fun if you leave the baskets open at the top so that little people can be popped inside and go ballooning.

Quiltsize: 54 × 47cm (21¼ × 18½in)
Pattern size: 23.5 × 17.5cm (9¼ × 7in)

Note

The directions refer to the top balloon, with the fabrics for the lower balloon given in brackets.

Method

1 Cut a 6cm (2½in) wide strip from the yellow fabric patterned with blue for section 17 and cut the remaining 14 × 12cm (5½ × 5in) into strips each measuring 4cm (1½in) wide. The fabric in the other three colours for the balloon filling must be uniformly cut into strips 4cm (1½in) wide.

2 Enlarge the pattern for the balloon on page 29 and then trace it, including the numbers, on to interfacing. Turn the interfacing over, lay the glossy fabric over the 'heart', right side up, and pin it in place. Turn your work over again and tack the glossy fabric on to the interfacing, just outside the stitching line. Turn your work over yet again and cut the glossy fabric into the rhomboid shape of the heart, leaving a small seam allowance all round.

3 Pin 5 × 4cm (2 × 1½in) of pale yellow and white patterned fabric (turquoise fabric) right side down over the heart by the stitching line of section 1, keeping the upper edge level with the edge of the silver (blue-and-green) glossy fabric. Turn your work over to the side bearing the numbers and sew the strip along the stitching line of section 1. Turn your work over

For each balloon
- 14 × 18cm (5½ × 7½in) of yellow fabric patterned with blue (turquoise fabric) • 15 × 16cm (5⅞ × 6in) of patterned blue (pink-and-red) fabric • 15 × 16cm (5⅞ × 6in) of pale yellow and white patterned fabric (turquoise fabric) • 10 × 16cm (4 × 6¼in) of dark blue (pink) fabric • 8 × 5.5cm (3¼ × 2¼in) of patterned blue (turquoise) fabric for the basket • 6 × 7cm (2½ × 2¾in) of silver (blue-and-green) glossy fabric • 25 × 20cm (10 × 8in) of lightweight white sew-in interfacing, e.g. Vilene L11 • Small figure (balloonist)

For the rest
- 45 × 37cm (17¾ × 14½in) of light blue fabric for the background sky • 47 × 10cm (18½ × 4in) of pink fabric for the narrow border • 48 × 18cm (19 × 7in) of patterned blue fabric for the outer border and 14 × 56cm (5½ × 22in) for the binding • 58 × 50cm (22¾ × 19¾in) of wadding (batting) • 58 × 50cm (22¾ × 19¾in) of fabric of your choice for the backing • Black embroidery cotton • 18mm (¾in) bias-binding maker

again and trim the seam allowance short. Open out the strip, press it flat and pin it to the next stitching line.

4 Pin 5 × 4cm (2 × 1½in) of patterned blue (pink-and-red) fabric right side down over the heart by the stitching line

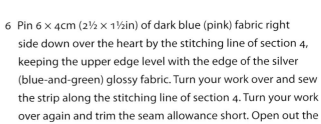

6 Pin 6 × 4cm (2½ × 1½in) of dark blue (pink) fabric right side down over the heart by the stitching line of section 4, keeping the upper edge level with the edge of the silver (blue-and-green) glossy fabric. Turn your work over and sew the strip along the stitching line of section 4. Turn your work over again and trim the seam allowance short. Open out the strip, press it flat and pin it to the next stitching line.

7 Repeat the procedure described above from step 3 onwards, with the same colour sequence and increasingly long strips on sections 5, 6, 7, 8, etc. For section 17, use the 6cm (2½in) wide yellow fabric patterned with blue (turquoise fabric) strip.

What to do next

1 Make the second balloon in the same way using the fabrics given in brackets. Using small stitches, tack around each balloon just outside the stitching line. Cut each balloon into shape, leaving a 6mm (¼in) seam allowance. Square off the edges along the hollow parts, going slightly inward and snip the seam allowance here for ease. Tack with small stitches just beyond the outline. Pull the tacking thread to fold the seam allowance to the back. Attach the right-hand balloon 3.5cm (1⅜in) from the upper edge and 6cm (2½in) from the right-hand edge of the light blue background fabric. Attach the left-hand balloon 11.5cm (4½in) from the upper edge and about 6cm (2½in) from the left-hand edge.

2 Fold the fabric for each basket in half, right sides together, so it is 4 × 5.5cm (1½ × 2¼in) and position the fold along the top. Sew the side edges together and turn the basket out. Fold a small seam allowance to the inside along the lower edge and pin the basket in place following the pattern.

of section 2, keeping the upper edge level with the edge of the silver (blue-and-green) glossy fabric. Turn your work over and sew the strip along the stitching line of section 2. Turn your work over again and trim the seam allowance short. Open out the strip, press it flat and pin it to the next stitching line.

5 Pin 6 × 4cm (2½ × 1½in) of pale yellow and white patterned fabric (turquoise fabric) right side down over the heart by the stitching line of section 3, keeping the upper edge level with the edge of the silver (blue-and-green) glossy fabric. Turn your work over and sew the strip along the stitching line of section 3. Turn your work over again and trim the seam allowance short. Open out the strip, press it flat and pin it to the next stitching line.

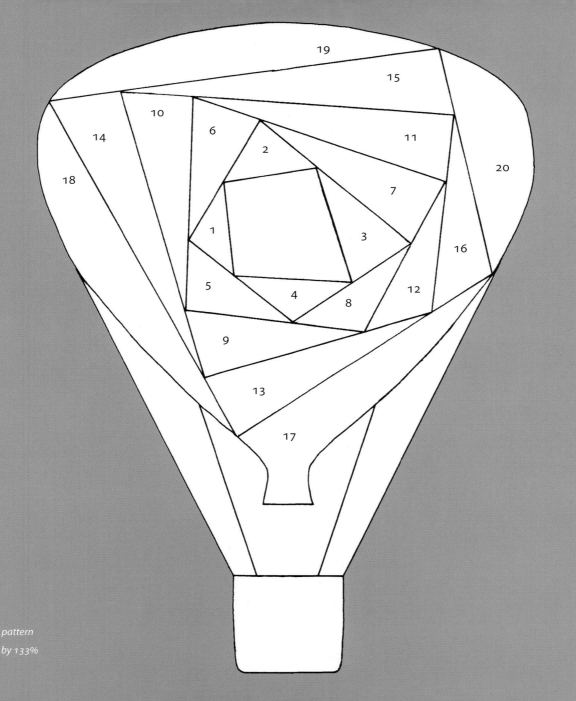

Balloon pattern
Enlarge by 133%

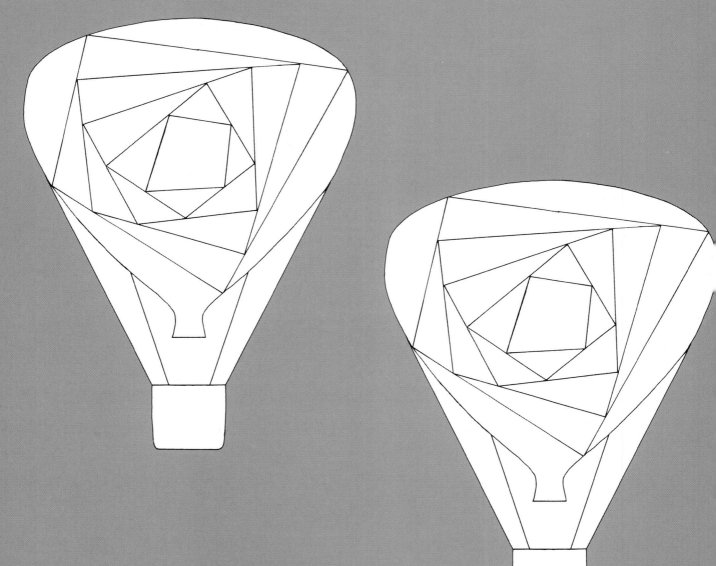

Balloon templates
Copy and colour in the templates with the colours of your fabrics

Attach the side and lower edges of the basket to the background fabric. Represent the ropes of the balloons with split-stitch embroidery.

Putting it all together

Cut the pink fabric for the narrow border into four strips, each 2.5cm (1in) wide. Sew a strip to each side and then to the upper and lower edges of the quilt. Cut the patterned blue fabric for the outer border into four strips 4.5cm (1¾in) wide and sew these on in the same way.

Finishing off

Make a quilt sandwich with the wadding between the top quilt and backing, right sides out, and tack the layers. Quilt around the balloons and baskets, adding 'clouds' in whatever form you like. Cut the binding fabric into four strips, each 3.5cm (1⅜in) wide, put them through the bias-binding maker and sew them to the outer border. Trim the quilt neatly and sew the binding tightly to the backing. Place your balloonists in the baskets.

An Apple a Day

Make good use of those fabric leftovers that you knew would come in handy one day by making this tasty-looking apple. It features almost twenty different fabrics, so plunge into your rag basket to find tones of red, yellow and green.

Quilt size: 31cm (12¼in) square
Pattern size: 14.5 × 15cm (5¾ × 6in)

Note

If you begin by copying and colouring the template on page 34 using the colours of your fabrics, you can see how your apple is going to look. Starting at the core, choose colours progressing from light to dark. The red fabric chosen is the same for both sides of the apple.

Method

1   Trace the pattern from page 34, including the numbers, on to interfacing. Turn the interfacing over, lay 5 × 4cm (2 × 1½in) of pale yellow fabric over the 'heart', right side up, and pin it in place. Turn your work over again and tack the piece of fabric to the interfacing, just outside the stitching lines. Turn your work over yet again and cut the fabric into the rhomboid shape of the heart, leaving a small seam allowance all round.

2   Pin 5 × 4cm (2 × 1½in) of the yellow fabric that comes next right side down over the heart by the stitching line of section 1, keeping the upper edge level with the edge of the pale yellow heart. Turn your work over to the side bearing the numbers and sew the strip along the stitching line of section 1. Turn your work over again and trim the seam allowance short. Open out the yellow strip, press it flat and pin it to the next stitching line.

For the apple
• Fabric strips 4cm (1½in) wide: six in varied shades of red, six in varied shades of green and seven in varied shades of yellow • 22cm (8¾in) square of lightweight white sew-in interfacing, e.g. Vilene L11

For the rest
• 22cm (8¾in) square of beige fabric for the background • 90 × 2.5cm (35½ × 1in) of green fabric for the narrow inner border • 110 × 5cm (43½ × 2in) of flowered beige fabric for the outer border • 4cm (1½in) square of brown felt • 34cm (13½in) square of wadding (batting) • 34cm (13½in) square of backing fabric • 130cm (51in) of wide red bias binding

3   Pin 5 × 4cm (2 × 1½in) of red fabric right side down over the heart by the stitching line of section 2, keeping the upper edge level with the edge of the pale yellow heart. Turn your work over and sew the strip along the stitching line of section 2. Turn your work over again and trim the seam allowance short. Open out the red strip, press it flat and pin it to the next stitching line.

4   Pin 4 × 4cm (1½ × 1½in) of green fabric right side down over the heart by the stitching line of section 3, keeping the upper edge level with the edge of the pale yellow heart. Turn

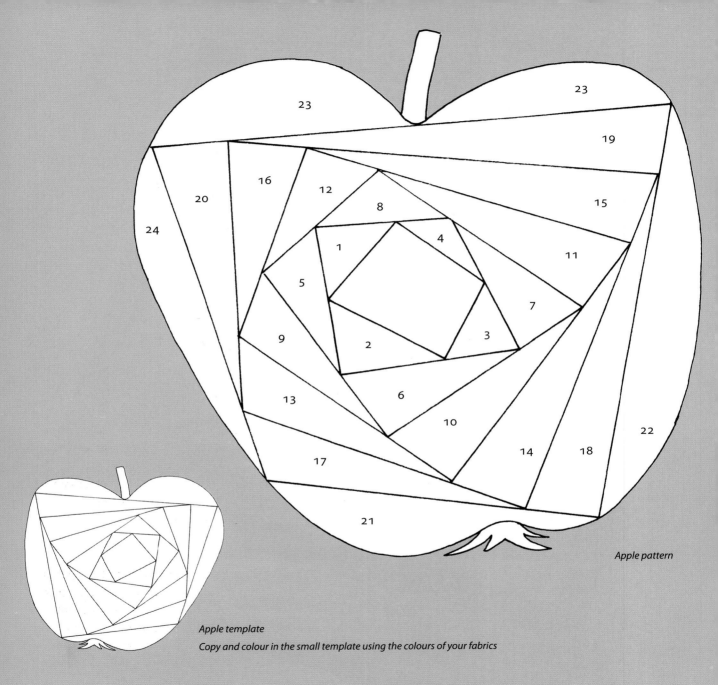

Apple pattern

Apple template
Copy and colour in the small template using the colours of your fabrics

your work over and sew the strip along the stitching line of section 3. Turn your work over again and trim the seam allowance short. Open out the green strip, press it flat and pin it to the next stitching line.

5 Pin 5 × 4cm (2 × 1½in) of red fabric right side down over the heart by the stitching line of section 4, keeping the upper edge level with the edge of the pale yellow heart. Turn your work over and sew the strip along the stitching line of section 4. Turn your work over again and trim the seam allowance short. Open out the red strip, press it flat and pin it to the next stitching line.

6 The first round is now finished. Leaving a small seam allowance, snip off any bits of fabric that are sticking out so that you can see which way the strips will go in the next round.

What to do next

Repeat the procedure described above from step 2 onwards with increasingly long strips in order to fill sections 5, 6, 7, etc. You will find the right measurements for the fabric by measuring on the pattern and adding a generous seam allowance. In the second round, you will use the second version of each colour, the third version in the third round, and so on. Tack the final strips just outside the stitching line.

Putting it all together

1 Once the apple is finished, trace the outline of the apple pattern in pencil on the back of the 22cm (8¾in) square of beige background fabric. Sew with the sewing machine in a zigzag just next to the pencil outline of the apple. Carefully cut out the apple shape inside the zigzag. Turn the fabric over and lay it over the apple so that the apple fits into the hole you have cut. Tack the apple firmly to the background and stitch it to the fabric with a wide zigzag on top of the first zigzag. Cut the apple's stalk and sepals out of felt and stitch these to the top and bottom of the apple.

2 Stitch the green inner border to the backing, starting with the pieces at the top and bottom and then adding the sides. Repeat with the outer border.

Finishing off

Make a quilt sandwich with the wadding between the top quilt and backing, right sides out, and tack the layers together. Quilt along the seams (stitch in the ditch) of each strip of the apple with matching quilting thread. Quilt around the apple and along the seams of the beige fabric and the green border. Trim the edges straight and finish off with red bias binding.

Spring Flowers

It can be spring in your home every day with this glorious quilt. Stunning red tulips with lush green leaves on a background of jumping lambs make this quilt a true harbinger of spring.

Quilt size: 32 × 47cm (12½ × 18½in)
Pattern size: 24 × 12cm (9½ × 4¾in)

Note

Tulip pattern A is for the outer tulips and pattern B for the central one. The directions refer to the right-hand tulip, which is made from the same range of fabrics as the other two.

Method

1 Enlarge the pattern for the tulips on page 38 and then trace the tulip head and the numbers from pattern A on to the interfacing. Turn the interfacing over, lay the 4cm (1½in) square of red glossy fabric right side up over the 'heart' and pin it in place. Turn your work over and tack the glossy fabric to the interfacing just outside the stitching lines of the heart. Turn your work over again and cut the glossy fabric into the lozenge shape of the heart, leaving a small seam allowance all round.

2 Pin 4 × 3cm (1½ × 1¼in) of orange-yellow fabric right side down over the heart by the stitching line of section 1, keeping the upper edge level with the edge of the red glossy fabric. Turn your work over and sew the strip along the stitching line of section 1. Turn your work over again and trim the seam allowance short. Open out the orange-yellow strip, press it flat and pin it to the next stitching line.

For each tulip
- 27 × 3cm (10½ × 1¼in) of four different fabrics in red, orange and pink • 4cm (1½in) square of red glossy fabric • 20 × 16cm (8 × 6¼in) of green fabric for the leaves and stalk • 12 × 8cm (4¾ × 3¼in) of lightweight white sew-in interfacing, e.g. Vilene L11

For the rest
- 35 × 50cm (13¾ × 19¾in) of light green fabric with a motif of little sheep for the background (remnants are used for this on the quilt shown in the photograph) • 35 × 50cm (13¾ × 19¾in) of spring-green fabric for the backing • 35 × 50cm (13¾ × 19¾in) of thin iron-on interfacing • 35 × 50cm (13¾ × 19¾in) of wadding (batting) • 165 × 4cm (65 × 1½in) of spring-green fabric for the binding • 18mm (¾in) bias-binding maker

3 Pin 3.5 × 3cm (1⅜ × 1¼in) of patterned red fabric right side down over the heart by the stitching line of section 2, keeping the upper edge level with the edge of the red glossy fabric. Turn your work over and sew the strip along

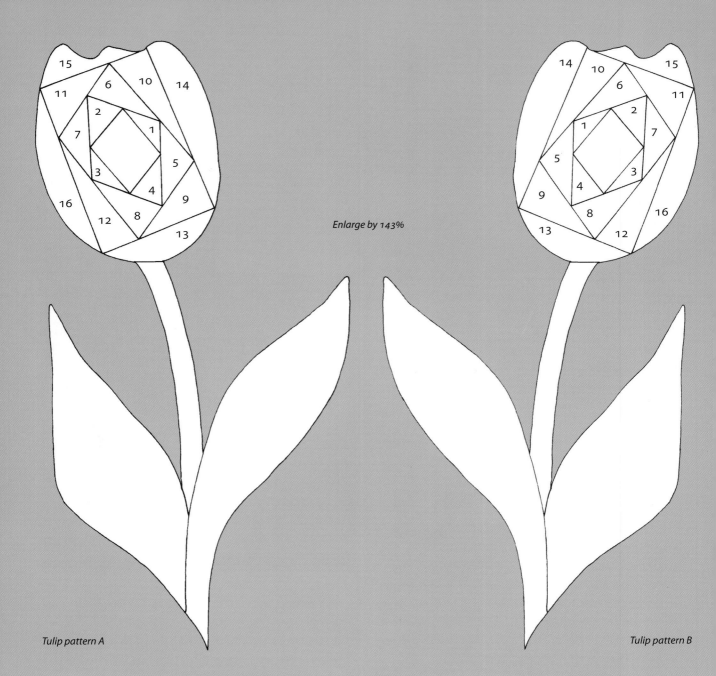

Enlarge by 143%

Tulip pattern A

Tulip pattern B

the stitching line of section 2. Turn your work over again and trim the seam allowance short. Open out the patterned red strip, press it flat and pin it to the next stitching line.

4 Pin 4 × 3cm (1½ × 1¼in) of pink fabric right side down over the heart by the stitching line of section 3, keeping the upper edge level with the edge of the red glossy fabric. Turn your work over and sew the strip along the stitching line of section 3. Turn your work over again and trim the seam allowance short. Open out the pink strip, press it flat and pin it to the next stitching line.

5 Pin 3.5 × 3cm (1⅜ × 1¼in) of orange fabric right side down over the heart by the stitching line of section 4, keeping the upper edge level with the edge of the red glossy fabric. Turn your work over and sew the strip along the stitching line of section 4. Turn your work over again and trim the seam allowance short. Open out the orange strip, press it flat and pin it to the next stitching line.

6 The first round is now complete. Leaving a seam allowance, snip off any bits of fabric that stick out so that you can see which way the strips will go in the next round.

What to do next

1 Repeat the procedure described above from step 2 onwards with increasingly long strips 3cm (1¼in) wide to fill sections 5, 6, 7, 8, etc. You will find the right measurements by measuring on the pattern and adding a generous seam allowance. In the second round, begin again with orange-yellow and then apply patterned red, then pink and then orange. Keep on alternating the four fabric colours as you sew, but always in the same order.

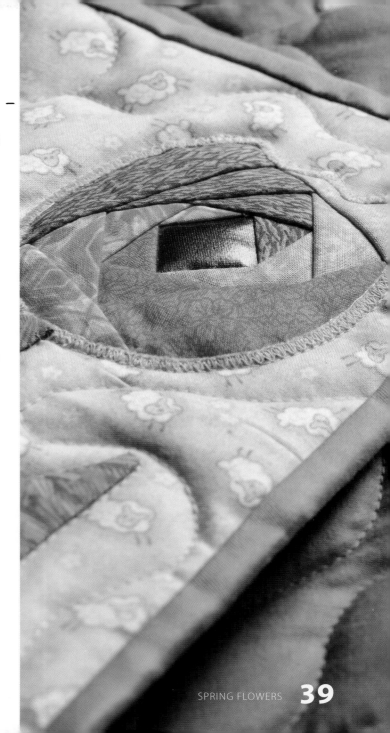

2 Make the left-hand tulip in the same way using four different orange fabrics. For the central tulip, follow pattern B and fill the flower head with four fabrics in colours ranging from pink to dark red.

Putting it all together

1 Reinforce the spring-green background fabric with the iron-on interfacing. Trace the mirror image of each tulip-head pattern on to the front of the fabric, with the top roughly 3cm (1¼in) from the upper edge. Measuring from the left-hand edge where the tulip heads are widest, the composition of the backing is roughly as follows: 7cm (2¾in) of background, orange tulip,

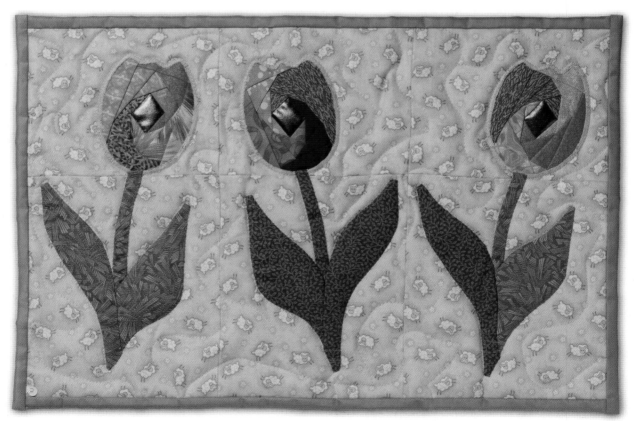

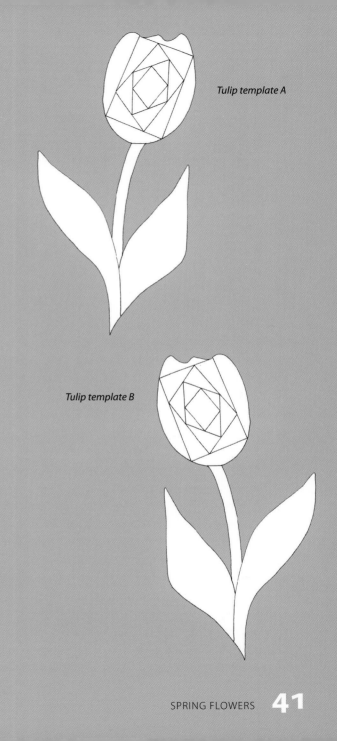

Tulip template A

Tulip template B

4cm (1½in) of background, pink-red tulip, 12cm (4¾in) of background, mixed tulip and then 3cm (1¼in) of background.

2 Using a sewing machine, zigzag just outside the pencilled outline of the right-hand tulip head, and cut out the resulting shape just inside the stitching. Lay the hole you have made exactly over the orange-red tulip head, pin it in place and stitch the tulip head and backing together with a wide zigzag stitch over the first zigzag. Snip off any loose ends at the edges of the flower.

3 Cut out the stalk and the two leaves from green fabric in mirror image of the pattern, adding a 6mm (¼in) seam allowance all round. Tack in the seam allowance all round and then pull up the thread so that the seam allowance folds to the back. First attach the stalk to the flower and background fabric and then sew on the smaller leaf on the right, followed by the larger leaf. Attach the other tulip heads, stalks and leaves in the same way.

Finishing off

Make a quilt sandwich with the wadding between the top quilt and backing, right sides out, and tack the layers. Machine stitch along the seam lines of the stalk, leaves and around the flower heads (stitch in the ditch). Quilt the design further if you wish. Trim the outer edges nice and straight. Using the bias-binding maker and the thin strips of fabric, make the binding and bind the edges.

In and Out and Round About

This clever quilt is based around six triangles, three with the fabric strips placed clockwise and three with them placed anticlockwise. The quilt shown on page 49 is a variation using six triangles all the same.

Quilt size: 58 × 53cm (22¾ × 21in)
Pattern size: 16.5 × 19cm (6½ × 7½in)

Method

1 Cut out four strips 3.5cm (1⅜in) wide, from the light blue, patterned white and blue fabrics. Trace the pattern for triangle A from page 46, including the numbers, on to the interfacing. Turn the interfacing over, lay the 4cm (1½in) square of red fabric right side up over the 'heart' and pin it in place. Turn your work over and tack the red fabric on to the interfacing just outside the stitching lines. Cut the red fabric into the triangular shape of the heart, leaving a small seam allowance all round.

2 For section 1, pin a strip of light blue fabric measuring 5 × 3.5cm (2 × 1⅜in) right side down over the heart by the stitching line of section 1, keeping the upper edge level with the edge of the red fabric. Turn your work over to the side bearing the numbers and sew the strip along the stitching line of section 1. Turn your work over again and trim the seam allowance short. Open out the light blue strip, press it flat and pin it on to the next stitching line.

3 For section 2, pin a strip of patterned white fabric measuring 5 × 3.5cm (2 × 1⅜in) right side down over the heart by the stitching line of section 2, keeping the upper edge level with the edge of the red fabric. Turn your work over to the side bearing the numbers and sew the strip along the stitching line of section 2. Turn your work over again and trim the

> **For each triangle**
> • 19 × 14cm (7½ × 5½in) each of light blue, patterned white and mid-blue fabrics • 4cm (1½in) square of red fabric • 20 × 22cm (8 × 8¾in) of lightweight white sew-in interfacing, e.g. Vilene L11
>
> **For the rest**
> • Two 12.4 × 21.2cm (4⅞ × 8⅜in) pieces of mid-blue fabric for the filling sections • 50 × 20cm (19¾ × 8in) of mid-blue fabric for the inner border and 60 × 28cm (23¾ × 11in) of the same fabric for the outer border • 48 × 12cm (19 × 5in) of patterned white fabric for the narrow band • 2.5m (2½yd) of wide mid-blue bias binding • 62 × 57cm (24½ × 22½in) of fabric of your choice for the backing • 62 × 57cm (24½ × 22½in) of wadding (batting)

seam allowance short. Open out the patterned white strip, press it flat and pin it on to the next stitching line.

4 For section 3, pin a strip of mid-blue fabric measuring 5 × 3.5cm (2 × 1⅜in) right side down over the heart by the stitching line of section 3, keeping the upper edge level with the edge of the red fabric. Turn your work over to the side bearing the numbers and sew the strip along the stitching line of section 3. Turn your work over again and trim the seam allowance short. Open out the blue strip, press it flat and pin it on to the next stitching line.

5 Repeat the procedure described above from step 2 onwards, measuring out a generous length of strip for each section you are going to cover. Follow the numbering and keep alternating the light blue, patterned white and mid-blue, always in the same sequence. Make another two triangles in the same way.

What to do next

1 Make three more triangles as described above but using pattern B (see page 47). The sequence of colours is the same as for pattern A.

2 Just outside the stitching lines, tack the last strips to the interfacing around all six of the triangles. Cut the triangles to shape, leaving a 6mm (¼in) seam allowance all round. Stitch the triangles together to form a hexagon, joining them blue against blue and patterned white against patterned white.

Putting it all together

1 Place the filling rectangles on top of each other with wrong sides facing and cut them diagonally in half into two positive and two negative filling pieces. Attach these triangles above and below the hexagon to form a rectangle. Assuming a seam allowance 1cm (⅜in) wide, there is enough material to trim the edges nice and square.

2 Cut the mid-blue fabric for the inner border into four strips, each 5cm (2in) wide. Sew a strip first to the upper and lower edges and then to the side edges. Cut the patterned white fabric for the narrow band into four strips, each 3cm (1¼in) wide, and sew them on in the same way. Cut the mid-blue fabric for the outer border into four strips 7cm (2¾in) wide. Sew these first to the sides, then to the upper and lower edges.

These versions have been handmade and quilted by Herma van Kampen, Tiny Meyerink, Rieny van Asselt, Harmke Wolters, Truus van Asch and Corrie Paat. Notice the clever border variations.

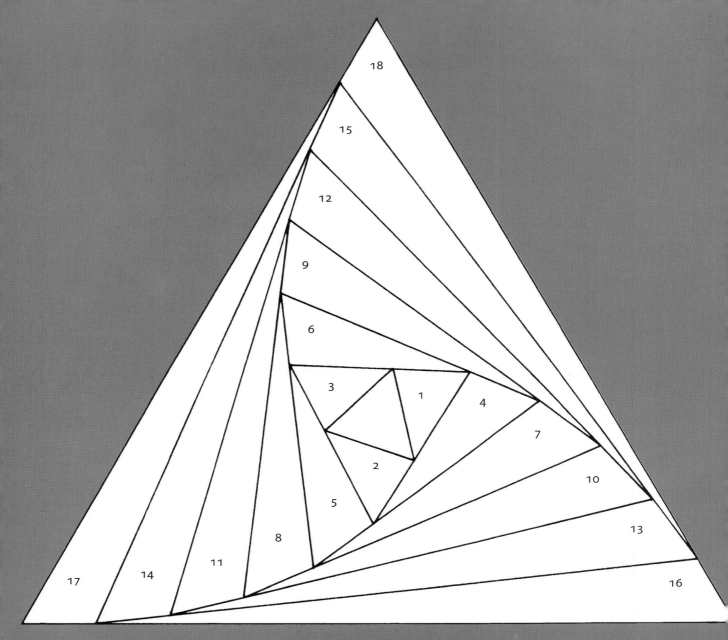

Triangle pattern A

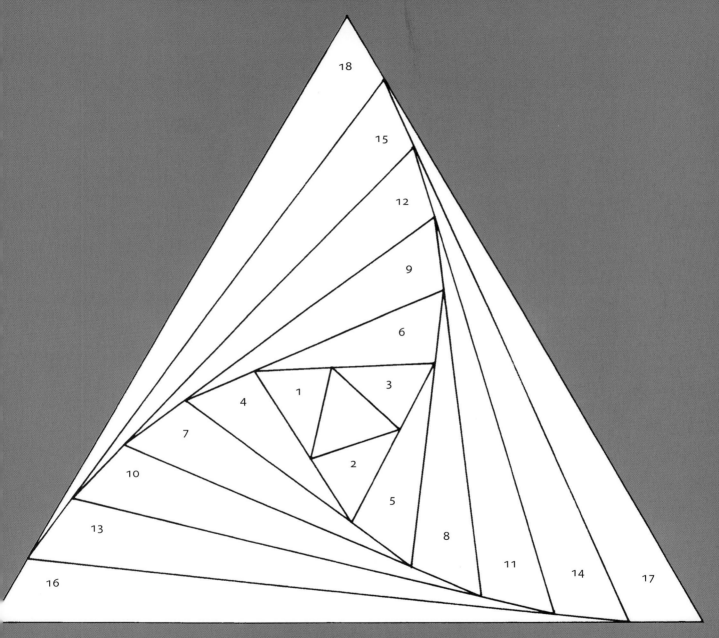

Triangle pattern B

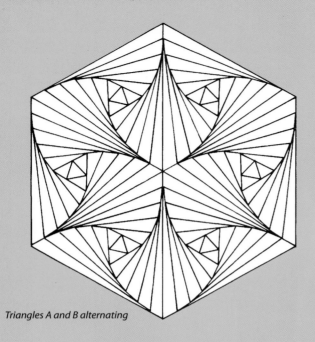

Triangles A and B alternating

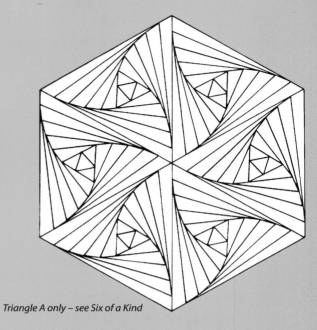

Triangle A only – see Six of a Kind

Finishing off

Iron the top quilt. Make a quilt sandwich with the wadding between the top quilt and backing, right sides out, and tack the layers. Stitch along the seams between the three colours of each triangle and around the edge of the hexagon. On the mid-blue corner triangles, stitch straight lines 2cm (¾in) apart. Quilt triangles into the outer border. Trim the quilt neatly and bind the edges.

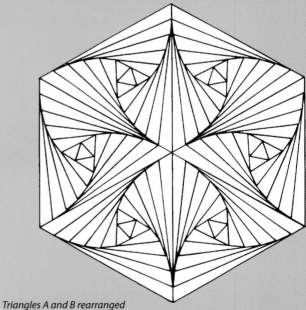

Triangles A and B rearranged

Copy and colour in the templates using the colours of your fabrics

Six of a Kind

Simply by dropping the second triangle from the previous quilt, a whole new look is achieved. The resulting pattern forms a windmill with a tremendous sense of flow and movement.

For each triangle
- 19 × 14cm (7½ × 5½in) each of yellow, multicoloured and red fabrics • 4cm (1½in) square of blue fabric • 20cm (8in) square of lightweight white sew-in interfacing, e.g. Vilene L11

For the rest
- Two 12.8 × 21.2cm (5 × 8⅜in) pieces of red fabric for the four filling pieces • 41 × 3cm (16¼ × 1¼in) and 33 × 3cm (13 × 1¼in) of red fabric for the narrow inner border • 48 × 20cm (19 × 8in) of yellow fabric for the outer border • 1.9m (2yd) of yellow satin bias binding • 52 × 47cm (20½ × 18½in) of yellow fabric for the backing • 52 × 47cm (20½ × 18½in) of wadding (batting)

Quilt size: 48 × 43cm (19 × 17in)
Pattern size: 16.5 × 19cm (6½ × 7½in)

Method

1 Cut four strips measuring 19 × 3.5cm (7½ × 1⅜in) from each of the triangle fabrics. Trace triangle A from page 46, including the numbers, on to the interfacing. Turn the interfacing over, lay the square of blue fabric over the 'heart' and pin it in place. Turn the interfacing over again and tack the fabric to the interfacing just outside the stitching lines of the heart. Turn your work over yet again and cut the fabric into the triangular shape of the heart, leaving a small seam allowance all round.

2 For all six triangles, follow the instructions for In and Out and Round About beginning on page 42. Work in the colour sequence yellow, multicolour and red.

What to do next

Tack the final strips of the triangles to the interfacing just outside the stitching lines and cut them into shape leaving a 6mm (¼in) seam allowance all round. Place the red points of all six triangles together and stitch the seams to join the triangles into a hexagon.

Putting it all together

1 Place the red rectangles for the filling pieces together with wrong sides facing and cut them diagonally in half into two positive and two negative filling pieces. Attach these triangles to the hexagon to make the quilt rectangular. Assuming a 1cm (⅜in) seam allowance, there is plenty of material to trim the edges nice and square.

2 Sew the narrow red border strips to the top and bottom edges and then to the sides. Cut the yellow fabric for the outer borders into four 5cm (2in) strips and attach these to the quilt in the same order as the inner border strips.

Finishing off

Iron the top quilt and then make a quilt sandwich with the wadding between the top quilt and backing, right sides out. Tack the layers together. Stitch along the seams between the three colours of each triangle by hand and stitch between the red border and the yellow one. Quilt the outer border in straight lines 5cm (2in) apart then trim the quilt neatly and attach the yellow satin bias binding.

Soaring into the Wind

Who, as a child, has not launched a kite into the wind? Recapture the memory using fabric, thread and interfacing instead of paper, glue, string and sticks. I hope you get as much pleasure out of these as you did from the real thing.

Quilt size: 65 × 50cm (25½ × 19¾in)
Pattern size: 18 × 12.5cm (7 × 5in) for the kite and 8.5 × 12.5cm (3⅜ × 5in) for the tail

Note

The kites consist of two different fabrics used alternately. The colours in brackets are for the topmost kite.

Method

1 Cut one strip of fabric measuring 15 × 5cm (6 × 2in) from colour 1 (plain yellow in the top kite) and set aside. Cut the remainder of colour 1 and all of colour 2 into strips measuring 15cm × 4cm (6 × 1½in) – you will need to trim the width of the final strip of colour 2.

2 Enlarge the pattern for the kite on page 55 and then trace the kite, including the numbers and letters, on to interfacing. Turn the interfacing over then lay the glossy fabric (golden yellow) right side up over the 'heart' and pin it in place. Turn your work over again and tack the glossy fabric to the interfacing just outside the stitching lines. Turn your work over yet again and cut the glossy fabric into the lozenge shape of the heart, leaving a small seam allowance all round.

3 For section 1, take a strip of colour 1 (plain yellow) measuring 5 × 4cm (2 × 1½in) and pin it right side down over the heart by the stitching line of section 1, keeping the upper edge level with the edge of the glossy fabric.

For each kite
- 15 × 29cm (6 × 11½in) of fabric in colour 1 and colour 2 plus remnants for the tail pennants • 32 × 18cm (12½ × 7in) of light blue fabric for the filling pieces and tail background • 6 × 4cm (2½ × 1½in) of glossy fabric • 20cm (8in) of red silk cord for the tail • 22 × 16cm (8¾ × 6¼in) of lightweight white sew-in interfacing, e.g. Vilene L11

For the rest
- 32 × 30cm (12½ × 12in) of light blue fabric for the four corner pieces • 60 × 10cm (23½ × 4in) of fabric for the narrow yellow border • 60 × 24cm (23½ × 9½in) of dark blue fabric for the outer border • 68 × 53cm (26¾ × 21in) of the fabric of your choice for the backing • 68 × 53cm (26¾ × 21in) of wadding (batting) • 2.4m (2¾yd) of dark blue bias binding

Turn your work over to the side bearing the numbers and sew the strip along the stitching line of section 1. Turn your work over again and trim the seam allowance short. Open out the (plain yellow) strip, press it flat and pin it to the next stitching line.

4 Pin a 5 × 4cm (2 × 1½in) strip of colour 2 (yellow butterfly pattern) right side down over the heart by the stitching line of section 2, keeping the upper edge level with the edge

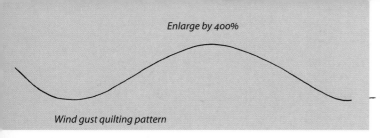

Enlarge by 400%

Wind gust quilting pattern

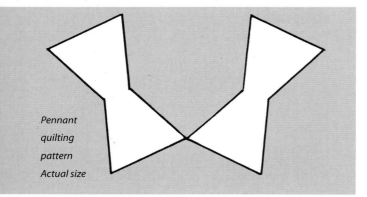

*Pennant
quilting
pattern
Actual size*

of the glossy fabric. Turn your work over to the side bearing the numbers and sew the strip along the stitching line of section 2. Turn your work over again and trim the seam allowance short. Open out the (yellow butterfly pattern) strip, press it flat and pin it on to the next stitching line.

5 Pin a 5 × 4cm (2 × 1½in) strip again of colour 1 (plain yellow) right side down over the heart by the stitching line of section 3, keeping the upper edge level with the edge of the glossy fabric. Turn your work over to the side bearing the numbers and sew the strip along the stitching line of section 3. Turn your work over again and trim the seam allowance short. Open out the (plain yellow) strip, press it flat and pin it on to the next stitching line.

6 Pin a 5 × 4cm (2 × 1½in) strip again of colour 2 (yellow butterfly pattern) right side down over the heart by the stitching line of section 4, keeping the upper edge level with the edge of the glossy fabric. Turn your work over to the side

bearing the numbers and sew the strip along the stitching line of section 4. Turn your work over again and trim the seam allowance short. Open out the (yellow butterfly pattern) strip, press it flat and pin it on to the next stitching line. The first round is now complete.

7 Repeat the procedure described above from step 3 onwards, measuring out a generous length of strip for each section you are going to cover. Follow the numbering and keep alternating colours 1 and 2. For section 17, use the special colour 1 strip measuring 15 × 5cm (6 × 2in).

What to do next

1 Cut and attach the filling pieces around the kite in the order A, B, C and D. Carefully iron the kite on the back.

2 Cut an 11 × 15cm (4¼ × 6in) rectangle of light blue fabric for the background to the kite tail. Cut a total of three 9 × 2.5cm (3½ × 1in) rectangles from remnants of fabrics 1 and 2 to make the three tail pennants. Fold each one in half lengthways and stitch the long edges together. Turn the tube right side out and fold the raw ends to the back, overlapping them to make a finished rectangle roughly 4 × 1cm (1½ × ⅜in). Secure the overlap then tie the pennants to each other with silk cord. Attach the blue rectangle to the bottom edge of the kite rectangle, catching in the top end of

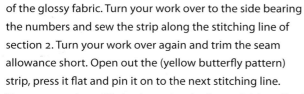

the cord, which should be positioned at the lower end of the kite and fastened at the back. Put the tail into position on the light blue background rectangle. Hold the tail in place by sewing the knots of cord behind the pennants on to the light blue fabric, working through from the back of the fabric.

3 Make the other three kites in the same way using your chosen colours.

Putting it all together

1 First put together two kite rectangles with their tails, which occupy the middle vertical, measuring 54.5 × 14cm (21½ × 5½in). Cut the fabric for the corner rectangles into four equal pieces. Make the outer verticals, which each consist of a corner rectangle, a kite rectangle and tail, and another corner rectangle, as shown in the template on page 56. Join all three verticals together.

2 Cut the yellow fabric into 2.5cm (1in) wide strips and join a strip to the top and bottom edges and then to the sides. Cut the dark blue fabric for the outer border into 6cm (2⅜in) wide strips and sew these on in the same way.

Finishing off

Iron the top quilt. Make a quilt sandwich with the wadding between the top quilt and backing, right sides out, and tack the layers together. Quilt the wind gusts – wavy lines 3cm (1¼in) apart – across the background but not over the kites (see the template on page 54), and quilt the pennants on the outer border using the full-size pattern on the same page. Trim the edges and then bind them.

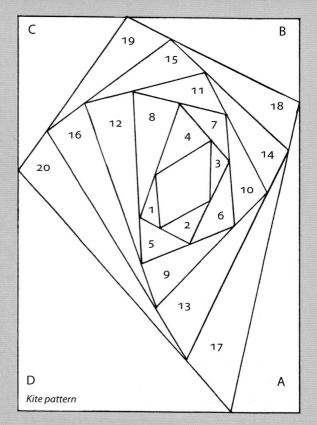

Kite pattern

Enlarge by 167%

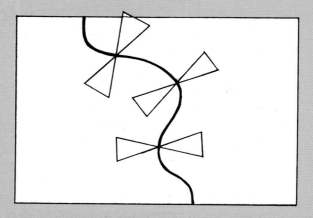

Template for the finished quilt

Copy and colour in the template using the colours of your fabrics

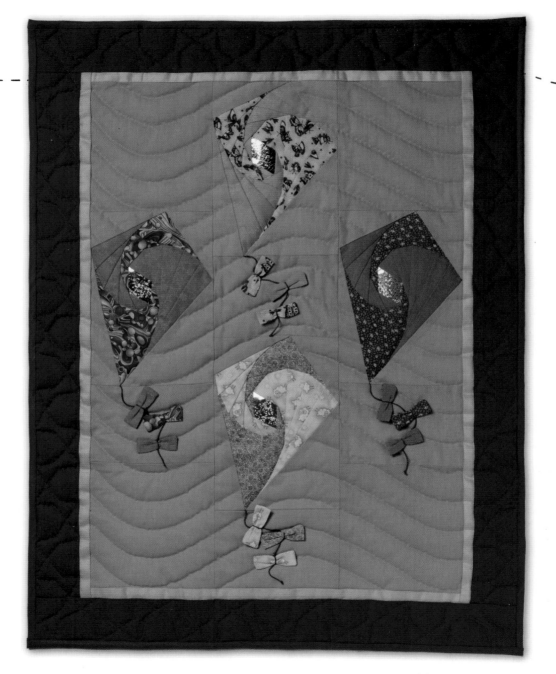

Topiary Trees

Use your creativity to decorate this topiary tree and its terracotta pot. Will your tree be ringed by hearts, butterflies or leaves like the ones shown here, or have you got other ideas? You could make a tree for a special person in their favourite colours or for a celebration – a Christmas version, for example.

Quilt size: 54 × 54cm (21¼in) square and 27 × 18cm (10⅝ × 7in) for each tree panel
Pattern size: 19.5 × 11.3cm (7¾ × 4½in)

Note

The directions refer to making the tree surrounded by butterflies in the centre of the top row, but the same basic method is used to make all the trees.

Method

1 Cut the four green fabrics into strips measuring 9 × 3cm (3½ × 1¼in). Trace the ball-shaped part of the tree from page 62, including the numbers, on to interfacing. Turn the interfacing over, lay the 4cm (1½in) square of green patterned fabric over the 'heart', right side up and pin it in place. Turn your work over again and tack the fabric to the interfacing, just outside the stitching lines. Turn your work over yet again and cut the fabric into the diamond shape of the heart, leaving a small seam allowance all round.

2 For section 1, take a strip of plain green fabric measuring 5 × 3cm (2 × 1¼in) and pin it right side down over the heart by the stitching line of section 1, keeping the upper edge level with the edge of the heart fabric. Turn your

For each tree
- 9 × 12cm (3½ × 5in) of fabric in plain green, dark green, light green and striped green • 4cm (1½in) square of green patterned fabric for the heart
- 5 × 2.5cm (2 × 1in) of patterned green fabric for the trunk • 8 × 10cm (3¼ × 4in) of terracotta fabric for the pot • 30cm (12in) of ribbon, 1.5cm (⅝in) wide • 5 butterfly stickers or other embellishments • 95cm (1yd) of brown bias binding • 30 × 20cm (12 × 8in) of ivory-white fabric with small green leaves for the background • 30 × 20cm (12 × 8in) of wadding (batting) • 30 × 20cm (12 × 8in) of fabric for the backing • 13cm (5in) square of lightweight white sew-in interfacing, e.g. Vilene L11

For the rest
For the other trees, the same quantities of material as given above, in four different patterns with four different shades of green • six hooks and eyes to join the panels • seven little green metal leaves for the tree shown bottom left • seven light green drawing-pin heads 1.3cm (½in) in diameter and 25 × 2.5cm (10 × 1in) of gold gauze binding for the tree shown top right • seven orange hearts and small beads for the tree shown top left • seven red paperclip wires for the tree shown bottom right • ivory-white quilting thread

work over to the side bearing the numbers, and sew the strip along the stitching line of section 1. Turn your work over again and trim the seam allowance short. Open out

the plain green strip, press it flat and pin it on to the next stitching line.

3 Pin a strip of dark green fabric measuring 5 × 3cm (2 × 1¼in) right side down over the heart by the stitching line of section 2, keeping the upper edge level with the edge of the heart fabric. Turn your work over to the side bearing the numbers and sew the strip along the stitching line of section 2. Turn your work over again and trim the seam allowance short. Open out the dark green strip, press it flat and pin it on to the next stitching line.

4 Pin a strip of light green fabric measuring 5 × 3cm (2 × 1¼in) right side down over the heart by the stitching line of section 3, keeping the upper edge level with the edge of the heart fabric. Turn your work over to the side bearing the numbers and sew the strip along the stitching line of section 3. Turn your work over again and trim the seam allowance short. Open out the light green strip, press it flat and pin it on to the next stitching line.

5 Pin a strip of striped green fabric measuring 5 × 3cm (2 × 3¼in) right side down over the heart by the stitching line of section 4, keeping the upper edge level with the edge of the heart fabric. Turn your work over to the side bearing the numbers and sew the strip along the stitching line of section 4. Turn your work over again and trim the seam allowance short. Open out the striped green strip, press it flat and pin it on to the next stitching line.

6 The first round is now finished. Repeat the procedure described above from step 2 onwards, measuring out a generous length of strip for each section you are going to cover. Follow the numbering and alternate the plain green, dark green, light green and striped green strips, in that order.

What to do next

1 Attach the last strips with tacking thread all round, just outside the stitching line. Cut out the circle with a 6mm (¼in) seam allowance and carefully pull on the tacking thread so that the seam allowance folds over to the back. Attach the round part of

the tree to the ivory-white background 6.5cm (2½in) from the top and 5.5cm (2¼in) from each side edge. Leave a little gap at the bottom so the 1cm (⅜in) wide trunk can slip underneath it.

2 Fold the long edges of the trunk piece to the back to make a trunk 1cm (⅜in) wide. Stitch it in place below the ball-shaped part of the tree, tucking the raw end underneath it, and sew down each long edge for 2.5cm (1in) – the gap at the bottom allows space for the bow. Turn all the edges to the back around the terracotta fabric to make the flowerpot shape and stitch it in place, allowing enough unstitched trunk above it for the ribbon to be threaded through.

Finishing off

1 Make a quilt sandwich with the wadding between the top quilt and backing, right sides out, and tack the layers. Attach the butterfly stickers then hand quilt around the whole tree and its pot. Quilt an outline around the round section and the butterflies. Trim the edges neatly and then bind them. Quilt the background 1cm (⅜in) away from the binding. Insert the ribbon through the gap behind the trunk just above the pot and tie it in a bow.

2 Make as many trees as you like using the photographs as a guide for the decorations or choosing your own colours and embellishments.

3 Sew sleeves on to the backs of the three top tree quilts so you can use a 54cm (21¼in) wooden dowel or pole with a diameter of 7mm (¼in) to hang them by. Arrange the trees in the right order and sew on the hooks and eyes so that the trees form a unified whole. Thread the pole through the sleeves.

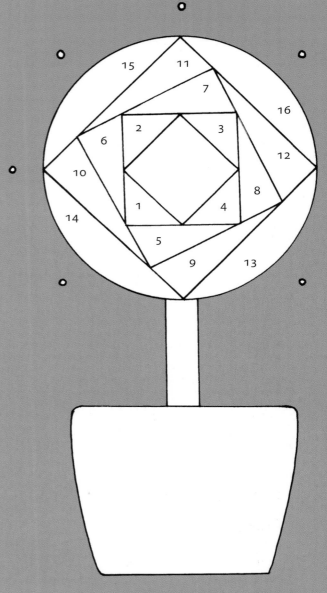

Tree pattern
Enlarge by 125%

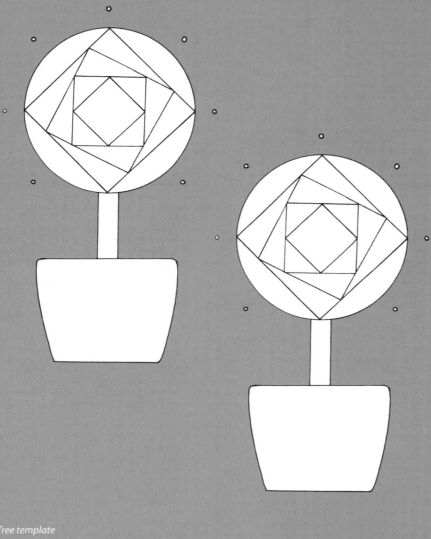

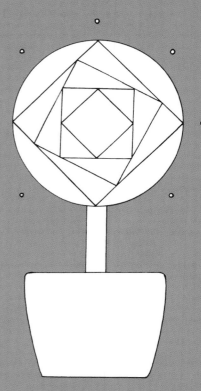

Tree template
Copy and colour in the template using the colours of your fabrics

Colour and Scent

If you enjoy a challenge, you will love making this quilt with its small bottles, each one using six different fabrics. For an easier option, you can enlarge the pattern and perhaps make an individual bottle quilt.

Quilt size: 21.5cm × 28cm (8½ × 11in)
Pattern size: 8cm × 5.8cm (3¼ × 2⅜in)

Method

1 Cut each of the fabrics in colours 1, 2 and 3 into four strips 2.5cm (1in) wide. Cut each of the fabrics in colours 4 and 5 into four strips 3cm (1¼in) wide.

2 Trace the bottle pattern from the top of page 66, including the numbers, on to interfacing using a sharp pencil. Turn the interfacing over, lay the glossy fabric, right side up, over the 'heart' and pin it in place. Turn your work over again and tack the glossy fabric to the interfacing just outside the stitching lines. Turn your work over yet again and cut the glossy fabric into the kite shape of the heart, leaving a small seam allowance all round.

3 For section 1, take a strip of colour 1 measuring 3 × 2.5cm (1¼ × 1in) and pin it right side down over the heart by the stitching line of

For each bottle
- 10cm (4in) square of fabric in colour 1 • 8 × 10cm (3¼ × 4in) of fabric in colour 2 • 9 × 10cm (3½ × 4in) of fabric in colour 3 • 11 × 12cm (4¼ × 5in) of fabric in colour 4 • 7 × 12cm (2¾ × 5in) of fabric in colour 5 • 3cm (1¼in) square of glossy fabric • 10cm (4in) square of lightweight white sew-in interfacing, e.g. Vilene L11 • 9 × 7.5cm (3½ × 3in) of fabric for the back of the bottle

For the rest
- 16.5 × 23cm (6½ × 9in) of lilac background fabric • 16.5 × 8cm (6½ × 9in) and 28 × 8cm (11 × 3¼in) of lilac pattern for the border • 25 × 32cm (10 × 12½in) of fabric for the backing • 25 × 32cm (10 × 12½in) of wadding (batting) • lilac, pink, purple and burgundy quilting thread • 104cm (41in) of lilac bias binding

section 1, keeping the upper edge level with the edge of the glossy fabric. Turn your work over to the side bearing the numbers and sew the strip along the stitching line of section 1. Turn your work over again and trim the seam allowance short. Open out the strip, press it flat and pin it on to the next stitching line.

4 For section 2, take a strip of colour 2 measuring 3 × 2.5cm (1¼ × 1in) and pin it right side down over the heart by the

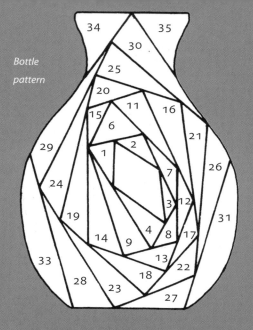

Bottle pattern

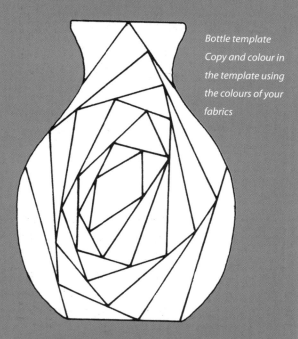

*Bottle template
Copy and colour in
the template using
the colours of your
fabrics*

stitching line of section 2, keeping the upper edge level with the edge of the glossy fabric. Turn your work over to the side bearing the numbers and sew the strip along the stitching line of section 2. Turn your work over again and trim the seam allowance short. Open out the strip, press it flat and pin it on to the next stitching line.

5 For section 3, take a strip of colour 3 measuring 3 × 2.5cm (1¼ × 1in) and pin it right side down over the heart by the stitching line of section 3, keeping the upper edge level with the edge of the glossy fabric. Turn your work over to the side bearing the numbers and sew the strip along the stitching line of section 3. Turn your work over again and trim the seam allowance short. Open out the strip, press it flat and pin it on to the next stitching line.

6 For section 4, take a strip of colour 4 measuring 4 × 3cm 1½ × 1¼in) and pin it right side down over the heart by the stitching line of section 4, keeping the upper edge level with the edge of the glossy fabric. Turn your work over to the side bearing the numbers and sew the strip along the stitching line of section 4. Turn your work over again and trim the seam allowance short. Open out the strip, press it flat and pin it on to the next stitching line.

Note: there is no section 5, so skip colour 5 at this point.

7 Repeat the procedure described above from step 3 onwards, measuring out a generous strip length for each section you are going to cover. Follow the numbering and keep to the same sequence of colours. Note that there is no section 10 in the second round, so leave out colour 5 again. It is only in the third round that colour 5 appears in section 15. In the last round, section 32 is missing, so omit colour 2 there.

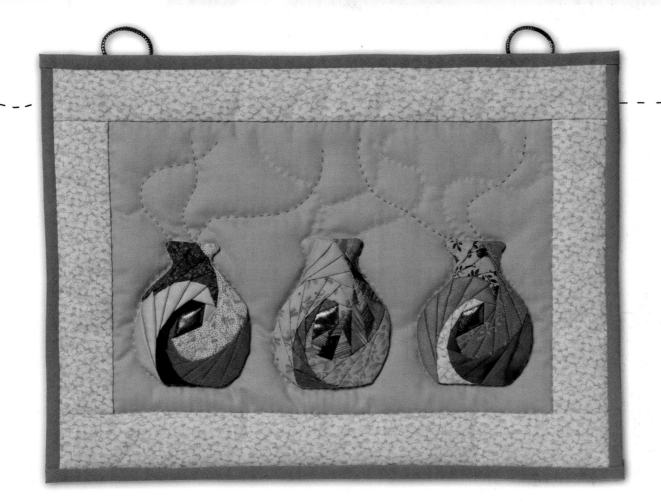

What to do next

Lay out the fabric for the back of the bottle, right side up. Lay the bottle on top, right side down, and stitch along the outline, hugging the pencil trace all the way. Trim the seam allowance short and snip it to the curves for ease. Cut a vertical slit in the back fabric only and turn the bottle out through it. With this finishing touch, all the loose ends will stay tucked away. Make two more bottles using different colours.

Finishing off

Pin and then stitch the bottles to the background fabric. Attach a patterned lilac border strip to each side and then to the top and bottom edges. Make a quilt sandwich with the wadding between the top quilt and backing, right sides out, and tack the layers. Choose quilting threads in suitable colours and hand quilt around the bottles, adding trails for the 'scents' above. Trim the quilt edges neatly and then bind them.

Sail Away

This fine yacht sails across the front of a smart clutch bag but you could easily make the design into a small quilt or combine several yachts in one quilt and create your own boat race.

Bag size: 22cm (8¾in) square
Pattern size: 15 × 14cm (6 × 5½in)

Method

1 Cut out five 3cm (1¼in) wide strips from the blue fabric, five patterned white strips and four green strips.

2 Trace the pattern for the boat from page 71, including the filling pieces, numbers and letters, on to the interfacing with a pencil. Turn the interfacing over, lay the glossy fabric, right side up, over the 'heart' and pin it in place. Turn your work over again and tack the glossy fabric to the interfacing just outside the stitching lines. Turn your work over yet again and cut the glossy fabric into the triangular shape of the heart, leaving a small seam allowance all round.

3 For section 1, pin a 6 × 3cm (2½ × 1¼in) strip of blue fabric right side down over the heart by the stitching line of section 1, keeping the upper edge level with the edge of the glossy fabric. Turn your work over to the side bearing the numbers and sew the strip along the stitching line of section 1. Turn your work over again and trim the seam allowance short. Open out the blue strip, press it flat and pin it on to the next stitching line.

4 For section 2, pin an 8 × 3cm (3¼ × 1¼in) strip of patterned white fabric right side down over the heart by the stitching line of section 2, keeping the upper edge level with the edge of the glossy fabric. Turn your work over to the side bearing the numbers and sew the strip along the stitching

For the yacht
- 10 × 15cm (4 × 6¼in) of blue fabric • 15cm (6¼in) square of patterned white fabric and 4 × 11.5cm (1½ × 4½in) of the same fabric for the hull (piece D) • 13 × 12cm (5¼ × 5in) of green fabric • 6 × 3cm (2½ × 1¼in) of silver glossy fabric • 18cm (7in) square of lightweight white sew-in interfacing, e.g. Vilene L11

For the front panel
- 14 × 18cm (5½ × 7in) of dark blue fabric for the filling pieces (A, B, C, E, F) • 17 × 11cm (6¾ × 4⅜in) for the two side filling pieces • 4 × 23cm (1½ × 9in) for the bottom filling piece

For the bag
- 46 × 23cm (18 × 9in) and 64 × 23cm (25¼ × 9in) of dark blue fabric • 18cm (7in) square of thin wadding (batting)

For the handle and clasp
- 40 × 5cm (15¾ × 2in) of dark blue fabric • 14cm (5½in) of blue cord • 22mm (¾in) dark blue button

line of section 2. Turn your work over again and trim the seam allowance short. Open out the patterned white strip, press it flat and pin it on to the next stitching line.

5 For section 3, pin a 4 × 3cm (1½ × 1¼in) strip of green fabric right side down over the heart by the stitching line

Yacht template
Copy and colour in the template using the colours of your fabrics

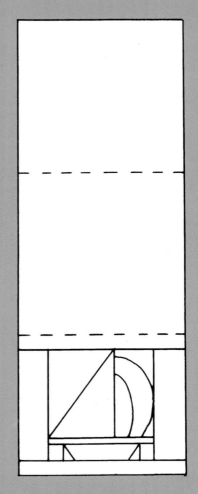

Clutch bag

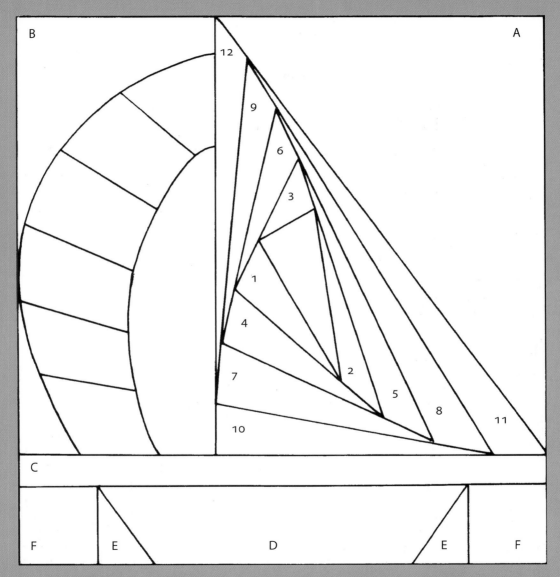

Yacht pattern

of section 2, keeping the upper edge level with the edge of the glossy fabric. Turn your work over to the side bearing the numbers and sew the strip along the stitching line of section 3. Turn your work over again and trim the seam allowance short. Open out the green strip, press it flat and pin it on to the next stitching line.

6 Repeat the procedure described above from step 3 onwards, measuring out a generous strip length for each section you are going to cover. Follow the numbering and use the same sequence of colours – blue, patterned white then green.

What to do next

1 For the front panel, stitch a dark blue triangle (filling piece A) on to the diagonal edge of the sail, so that your work measures 14 × 10.5cm (5½ × 4¼in). Press the panel carefully.

2 Cut out the pieces of fabric for the spinnaker (curving front sail) following the pattern and sew them to each other in order. Attach these pieces to filling piece B and to the other two dark blue shapes behind the spinnaker. Stitch the rectangle on to the long straight side of the sail, so that your work now measures 14 × 15.5cm (5½ × 6¼in). Attach filling piece C to the bottom edge.

3 Take the patterned white fabric for the hull of the boat and trim the ends on a slant following pattern D but remembering to add seam allowances. Cut out two small triangles of dark blue fabric for E and stitch them on to the prow and stern of the boat. Attach a 3.5 × 3cm (1⅜ × 1¼in) rectangle of dark blue fabric to each end of the hull section. Stitch the entire strip on to the interfacing under C.

Putting it all together

1 Cut the 17 × 11cm (6¾ × 4½in) rectangle of the dark blue fabric in half to make two equal pieces measuring 17 × 5.5cm (6¾ × 2¼in) and stitch them on to each side of the quilt. Stitch the 4 × 23cm (1½ × 9in) strip of dark blue fabric to the lower edge. Stitch 46 × 23cm (18 × 9in) of dark blue fabric across the upper edge. All this forms the outside of the bag.

2 Lay out the entire piece on your worktable, right side up, with the long edges at the side, and lay the 64 × 23cm (25¼ × 9in) rectangle of dark blue fabric right side down on top with raw edges matching. Cut the cord in half and fold one half to make a loop, slipping it between the layers at the bottom edge with the main part of the loop between the fabrics (at the end beneath the boat). Stitch the lower edge, catching the cord in the stitching to make a button loop. Tack the wadding to the back of the yacht then stitch the long side seams. Turn the bag right side out and press it.

Finishing off

Choose an appropriate machine stitch and work it 3mm (⅛in) around the yacht and between the sail and spinnaker. Fold in the seam allowances at the open end and stitch the opening closed. Fold the bag so the flap is 21cm (8¼in) and double-stitch the side edges together, catching in a second cord loop for the handle. Attach the button. Fold the handle strip lengthways, folding in the raw edges and stitch. Thread the handle through the side cord loop and stitch its ends firmly together.

Whirlwind

Pink fabrics, ranging from light to dark, spiral outwards on each of four squares, creating a huge amount of energy and movement when set against a dramatic black contrast. Arranged with the darkest pink strips touching, the effect is that of a whirlwind or vortex.

Quilt size: 40cm (15¾in) square
Pattern size: 12cm (4¾in) square

Method

1 Trace the whirlwind pattern from page 77, including the numbers, on to interfacing. Turn the interfacing over, cover the diamond-shaped 'heart' with the square of white fabric with black dots, right side up, and pin it in place. Turn your work over again and tack the fabric to the interfacing just outside the stitching lines. Turn your work over yet again and trim the seam allowance short.

2 Pin the lightest strip of pink fabric – measuring 5 × 3.5cm (2 × 1⅜in) – right side down over the heart by the stitching line of section 1, keeping the upper edge level with the edge of the heart fabric. Turn your work over to the side bearing the numbers and sew the strip along the stitching line of section 1. Turn your work over again and trim the seam allowance short. Open out the strip, press it flat and pin it on to the next stitching line.

3 Pin the lightest shaded strip of black-patterned fabric, cut to 5 × 3.5cm (2 × 1⅜in) right side down over the heart by the stitching line of section 2, keeping the upper edge level with the edge of the heart fabric. Turn your work over to the side bearing the numbers and sew the strip along the stitching line of section 2. Turn your work over again and trim the seam allowance short.

For each square
• Six variegated strips of pink fabric 3.5cm (1⅜in) wide, ranging from light to dark and respectively 5cm (2in), 6cm (2½in), 7cm (2¾in), 9cm (3½in), 11cm (4⅜in) and 12cm (4¾in) long • Six variegated strips of black-patterned fabric 3.5cm (1⅜in) wide, ranging from light to dark and respectively 15cm (6in), 18cm (7in), 21cm (8¼in), 27cm (10½in), 33cm (13in) and 36cm (14¼in) long • 4.5cm (1¾in) square of white fabric with black dots for the heart • 15cm (6in) square of lightweight white sew-in interfacing, e.g. Vilene L11

For the rest
• 30 × 14cm (12 × 5½in) of black fabric for the inner border • 32 × 10cm (12½ × 4in) of patterned pink fabric for the pink band • 43 × 26cm (17 × 10in) of black fabric for the outer border • 44cm (17½in) square of wadding (batting) • 44cm (17½in) square of the fabric of your choice for the backing • 175cm (69in) of black bias binding

Open out the strip, press it flat and pin it on to the next stitching line.

4 Pin another strip of the black-patterned fabric cut to 5 × 3.5cm (2 × 1⅜in) right side down over the heart by the stitching line of section 3, keeping the upper edge level

with the edge of the heart fabric. Turn your work over to the side bearing the numbers and sew the strip along the stitching line of section 3. Turn your work over again and trim the seam allowance short. Open out the strip, press it flat and pin it on to the next stitching line.

5 Pin a third strip of the black-patterned fabric measuring 5 × 3.5cm (2 × 1⅜in) right side down over the heart by the stitching line of section 4, keeping the upper edge

level with the edge of the heart fabric. Turn your work over to the side bearing the numbers and sew the strip along the stitching line of section 4. Turn your work over again and trim the seam allowance short. Open out the strip, press it flat and pin it on to the next stitching line. In this way, sections 2, 3 and 4 are covered with the same fabric.

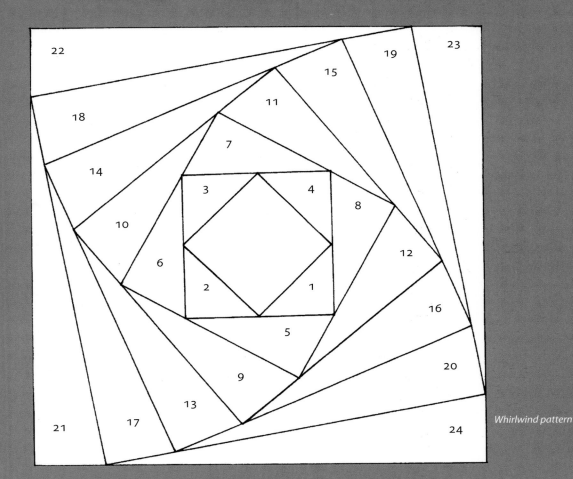

Whirlwind pattern

6 The first round is now complete. Leaving a seam allowance, snip off any bits that are sticking out so that you can see which way the strips go in the next round.

What to do next

Repeat the procedure described above from step 2 onwards with increasingly long strips in order to fill sections 5, 6, 7, etc. You will find the right measurements for the fabric by measuring on the pattern. In the 2nd round, use the next shade of pink and then the next shade of black three times in a row, and so on, continuing outwards all the time from lighter to darker. When all the sections are covered, tack the last strips to the interfacing just outside the stitching lines and cut the square into shape, leaving a 6mm (¼in) seam allowance all round. Make three more squares in the same way.

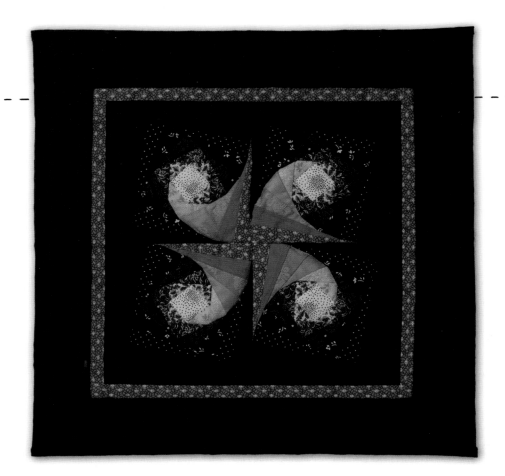

Putting it all together

1 Sew the squares together so that the dark pink fabrics meet in the middle (see the template on page 76).

2 Cut the black fabric for the inner border into four strips, each 3.5cm (1⅜in) wide. Sew one on to each side and then to the top and bottom edges. Cut the fabric for the pink band into four strips, each 2.5cm (1in) wide. Sew them on first to the sides, then to the top and bottom edges. Cut the black fabric for the outer border into four strips, each 6.5cm (2½in) wide. Sew them on first to the sides, then to the top and bottom edges.

Finishing off

Make a quilt sandwich with the wadding between the top quilt and backing, right sides out, and tack the layers together. Hand quilt the squares in whatever way you like. Machine a decorative stitch on to the two black borders. The quilting stitch used here is No. 45 from Pfaff Expression 2.0. Sew the bias binding on to the front side and trim the edge of the quilt neatly to fit. Hand-sew the bias binding to the back with small stitches.

A Rose for all Seasons

Whereas the other iris quilts have spiral designs, here we see distinct rings, characteristic of the queen of flowers. This is achieved by covering all the sections in each round with strips of the same fabric. Make the flower head using eight fabrics arranged from light in the centre to dark at the edges.

Quilt size: 30 × 20cm (12 × 8in)
Pattern size: 19.7 × 12cm (7¾ × 4¾in)

Method

1 Enlarge the rose pattern from page 82 and trace it on to interfacing, including the numbers. Turn the interfacing over, cover the 'heart' with the yellow fabric, right side up, and pin it in place. Turn your work over again and tack the fabric to the interfacing just outside the stitching lines. Turn your work over yet again and trim the seam allowances short.

2 Cut each of the colour 1 and colour 2 fabrics into three strips 2cm (¾in) wide. For section 1, pin a colour 1 strip measuring 3 × 2cm (1¼ × ¾in) right side down over the heart by the stitching line of section 1, keeping the upper edge level with the edge of the heart fabric. Turn your work over to the side bearing the numbers and sew the strip along the stitching line of section 1. Turn your work over again and trim the seam allowance

For the rose
- 4cm (1½in) square of yellow fabric • Seven variegated orange and red fabrics, ranging from light to dark outwards from the centre: 7 × 6cm (2¾ × 2¼in) in colour 1 and colour 2; 9 × 7.5cm (3½ × 3in) in colour 3 and colour 4; 12 × 7.5cm (4¾ × 3in) in colour 5 and colour 6, and 14 × 18cm (5½ × 7⅛in) in colour 7 • 20 × 1cm (8 × ⅜in) and 12.5 × 9cm (5 × 3½in) of green for the stalks and the leaves • 12cm (4¾in) of lightweight white sew-in interfacing, e.g. Vilene L11

For the rest
- 26 × 16cm (10¼ × 6¼in) and 14cm (5½in) square of fabric with an ivory-white leaf pattern for the background and as strengthening for the rose • 32 × 16cm (12½ × 6in) and 33 × 23cm (13 × 9in) of patterned orange fabric for the borders and the backing • 33 × 23cm (13 × 9in) of wadding (batting)

short. Open out the strip, press it flat and pin it on to the next stitching line. Fill the other no. 1 sections with colour 1 fabric in the same way.

3 Sew a colour 2 strip measuring 3.5 × 2cm (1⅜in × ¾in) to every section numbered 2 in the same way as the previous strips.

4 Cut each of the colour 3 and colour 4 fabrics into three strips 2.5cm (1in) wide. Sew a colour 3 strip measuring 4 × 2.5cm (1½ × 1in) on to each section numbered 3. Sew a colour 4 strip measuring 4.5 × 2.5cm (1¾ × 1in) on to each section numbered 4 in the same way.

5 Cut each of the colour 5 and colour 6 fabrics into three strips 2.5cm (1in) wide. Sew a colour 5 strip measuring 5 × 2.5cm (2 × 1in) on to each section numbered 5. Sew a colour 6 strip measuring 6 × 2.5cm (2½ × 1in) on to each section numbered 6 in the same way.

6 Cut the colour 7 fabric into three strips, each 6cm (2⅜in) wide and cut each strip in half to make strips 7 × 6cm (2¾ × 2⅜in). Fold each strip in half, right sides together, to measure 7 × 3cm (2¾ × 1 3/16in) and trace on to it the shape of each outer petal (section 7). Leave a 3mm (⅛in) seam allowance free at the bottom (straight) edge, to be stitched later. Sew along the shaped line, leaving the straight edge open, then trim the seam allowance short and turn each petal right side out. Sew the petals to the flower along the stitching line of each section 7, using the extra allowance and leaving the outer side free.

Putting it all together

1 Spread out the background fabric on your worktable, right side up and lay the small square of background material on top, wrong side up, so that its centre is 8cm (3¼in) from the top and 7.5cm (3in) from the right-hand edge. Tack the layers together round the borders of the square. Trace the pentagon pattern (the mirror image and other side of the 'rose' pattern) in the middle with pencil. Sew the fabric pieces together just inside

Rose template
Copy and colour in the template using the colours of your fabrics

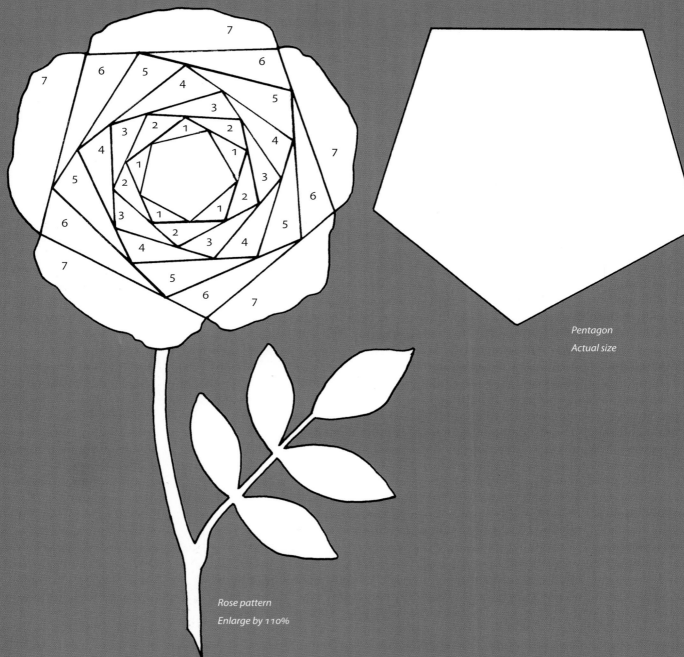

7

6
7   6
   6   5   5
            4   3
         3   4
      3   2   1   2
   4   2   1   1   2   4
      5   1   3
                                            7
   5   2   1   2
      6   3   6
                2   3   4
         7   5   4
                    6   5
                         7

Pentagon
Actual size

Rose pattern
Enlarge by 110%

the pencilled lines. Cut out the fabric inside the pentagon, but leaving a narrow seam allowance. Snip the seam allowance carefully at the corners, remove the tacking threads and turn the small piece through the opening to the back of the larger piece of fabric. Iron the seam flat.

2 Position the fabric with the pentagonal hole over the rose and bring up the outermost petals through the hole. Pin them in place and sew them on to the backing, except for the lower right-hand corner of section 7 on account of the stalk.

3 Fold the green fabric in half, wrong sides facing, and trace each leaf pattern on top. Sew around each leaf then trim the seam allowance very short. Make snips in the seam allowance at the angles, being careful not to cut the stitching, and turn the leaves out carefully. Roll up the long strip of fabric for the stem and sew on a 12cm (4¾in) length below the rose, attaching the upper end under the last red petal. Use 6cm (2½in) of the rolled fabric as the leaf stalk, slipping the ends of the leaves underneath it and attaching them at the same time.

Finishing off

1 Cut the smaller piece of patterned orange fabric into two strips measuring 32 × 4cm (12½ × 1½in) and two strips measuring 22 × 4cm (8¾ × 1½in). Sew them to your work, mitring the corners (see Techniques, page 8).

2 Spread out the fabric for the backing, right side up on your worktable, lay the rose right side down on top and then arrange the wadding on top of that. Sew tightly all round, leaving 14cm (5½in) open at the bottom. Cut away the wadding outside the seams. Turn the fabric out, tuck in a seam allowance along the bottom edge and stitch the gap

closed. Hand quilt around the rose and leaves and along the stalk and the border.

The Perfect Pear

This single fruit is quick to make and beautiful to behold. You could make the apple on page 32 as well, if you wish, using the same colours and border fabrics or even make a golden pear in yellows, ochre and brown.

Quilt size: 33 × 26cm (13 × 10¼in)
Pattern size: 19.7 × 11.5cm (7¾ x4½in)

Method

1 Trace the pear pattern from page 86, including the numbers, on to interfacing. Turn the interfacing over, cover the 'heart' with the green glossy fabric, right side up, and pin it in place. Turn your work over again and tack on the fabric to the interfacing just outside the stitching line. Turn your work over yet again and trim the fabric into the lozenge shape of the heart, leaving a small seam allowance all round.

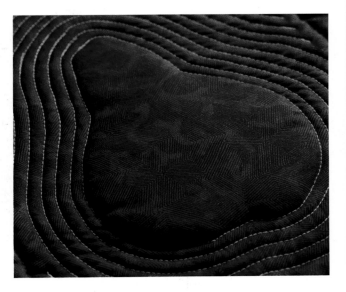

2 Cut all the green fabrics for filling the pear into strips, each 3.5cm (1⅜in) wide.

3 Pin 5.5 × 3.5cm (2¼ × 1⅜in) of the flowered green fabric right side down over the heart by the stitching line of section 1, keeping the upper edge level with the edge of the glossy fabric. Turn your work over to the side bearing the numbers and sew the strip along the stitching line of

For the pear filling
• 13 × 14cm (5¼ × 5½in) of flower-patterned green fabric • 13 × 14cm (5¼ × 5½in) of dark green fabric
• 16 × 14cm (6¼ × 5½in) of greyish green fabric
• 19 × 14cm (7½ × 5½in) of light green fabric • 5 × 3cm (2 × 1¼in) of green glossy fabric

For the rest
• 27 × 20cm (10¾ × 8in) of white fabric for the background
• 27 × 8cm (10¾ × 3in) of red fabric for the narrow border
• 28 × 16cm (11 × 6in) of white fabric with red dots for the wide border • Two strips 33 × 3.5cm (13 × 1⅜in) and two strips 28 × 3.5cm (11 × 1⅜in) of white fabric for the binding • 4 × 3cm (1½ × 1¼in) of brown felt • 36 × 29cm (14¼ × 11½in) of wadding (batting) • 36 × 29cm (14¼ × 11½in) of red fabric for the backing • 20 × 15cm (8 × 6in) of lightweight white sew-in interfacing, e.g. Vilene L11 • 18mm (¾in) bias-binding maker

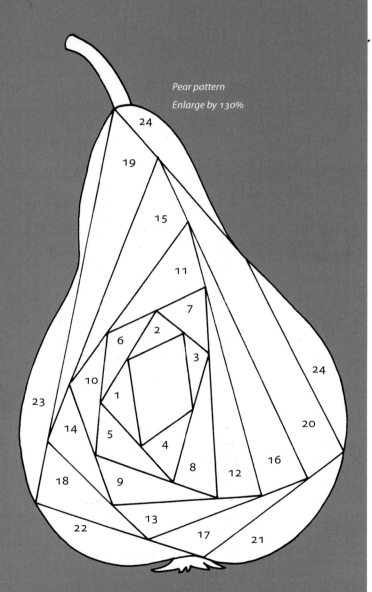

Pear pattern
Enlarge by 130%

section 1. Turn your work over again and trim the seam allowance short. Open out the flowered green strip, press it flat and pin it on to the next stitching line.

4 Pin 4 × 3.5cm (1½ × 1⅜in) of dark green fabric right side down over the heart by the stitching line of section 2, keeping the upper edge level with the edge of the glossy fabric. Turn your work over to the side bearing the numbers and sew the strip along the stitching line of section 2. Turn your work over again and trim the seam allowance short. Open out the dark green strip, press it flat and pin it on to the next stitching line.

5 Pin 4.5 × 3.5cm (1¾ × 1⅜in) of the greyish green fabric right side down over the heart by the stitching line of section 3, keeping the upper edge level with the edge of the glossy fabric. Turn your work over to the side bearing the numbers and sew the strip along the stitching line of section 3. Turn your work over again and trim the seam allowance short. Open out the greyish green strip, press it flat and pin it on to the next stitching line.

6 Pin 4 × 3.5cm (1½ × 1⅜in) of light green fabric right side down over the heart by the stitching line of section 4, keeping the upper edge level with the edge of the glossy fabric. Turn your work over to the side bearing the numbers and sew the strip along the stitching line of section 4. Turn your work over again and trim the seam allowance short. Open out the light green strip, press it flat and pin it on to the next stitching line.

7 The first round is now complete. Leaving a seam allowance, snip off any bits that are sticking out so you can see which way the strips go in the next round.

What to do next

Repeat the procedure described above from step 3 onwards with increasingly long strips in order to fill sections 5, 6, 7, etc. You will find the right sizes by measuring on the pattern and adding a generous seam allowance. In the 2nd round, use a strip of the flowered green fabric, then dark green, then greyish green, then light green – the sequence of colours is the same each time. Note that section 24 consists of two short strips.

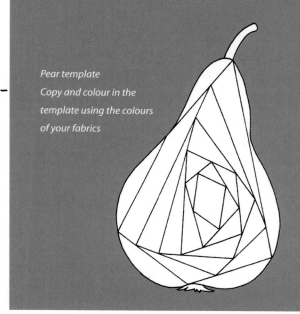

Pear template
Copy and colour in the template using the colours of your fabrics

Putting it all together

Tack all around the pear, just outside the stitching line. Cut out the pear with a 6mm (¼in) seam allowance all round. Pull the tacking thread so that the allowance folds over to the back along the curved lines, and stitch the pear on to the white background fabric.

Finishing off

Cut the red fabric for the narrow border into four strips 2cm (¾in) wide. Attach a strip to each side, then the top and bottom. Cut the white fabric with red dots for the wide border into four strips 4cm (1½in) wide. Attach a strip to each side, then to the top and bottom. Make a quilt sandwich with the wadding between the top quilt and backing, right sides out, and tack the layers. Machine stitch with a suitable stitch around the pear at a distance of about 7mm (¼in) and then work in parallel rows placed equidistantly outwards. Cut the stalk and sepals out of brown felt and stitch them on. Put the strips for the binding through the bias-binding maker and use them to finish the edges.

Light your Way

This spectacular finale is a fitting tribute to the skills you have learnt in the course of this book. Rich, dark fabrics with gold patterning set off the yellows of this lamp and its sparking heart, creating an eye-catching combination that will not fail to claim attention.

Quilt size: 38 × 37cm (15 × 14½in)
Pattern size: 23.5 × 15.8cm (9¼ × 6¼in)

Note
Sections 2, 6, etc. and 4, 8, etc. have a double covering, first with the narrow light yellow ray, then with the chosen fabric colour.

Method
1. Cut each of the four fabrics for the lantern into three strips measuring 20 × 4cm (8 × 1½in). Cut the light yellow fabric for the narrow intermediate strips into five strips measuring 36 × 2cm (14¼ × ¾in). Enlarge the lantern pattern from page 94 and trace it on to interfacing, including the letters and numbers. Turn the interfacing over, cover the 'heart' with the gold-coloured fabric, right side up, and pin it in place. Turn your work over again and tack the fabric just outside the stitching lines. Turn your work over yet again and trim the fabric into the diamond shape of the heart, leaving a small seam allowance all round.

2. For section 1, take a strip of dark yellow fabric measuring 6 × 4cm (2⅜ × 1½in) and pin it right side down over the heart by section 1. Turn your work over and sew the strip along the stitching line of section 1. Turn your work over again and trim the seam allowance short. Open out the strip of fabric, press it flat and pin it on to the next stitching line.

3. For section 2, first take an intermediate strip of light yellow fabric measuring 5 × 2cm (2 × ¾in) and pin it right side

For the lantern
- 20 × 12cm (8 × 4½in) of fabric in dark yellow, beige, patterned yellow and starred white • 5cm (2in) square of gold-coloured fabric or holographic paper • 36 × 10cm (14¼ × 3¾in) of light yellow fabric for all the narrow intermediate strips • 14 × 18cm (5½ × 7in) and 5 × 3.5cm (2 × 1⅜in) of beige-motif fabric for the lantern lid and tab • 3.5cm (1⅜in) brass ring • 18cm (7in) square of lightweight white sew-in interfacing, e.g. Vilene L11

For the rest
- 20 × 28cm (8 × 11in) of Vilene L11 lightweight white sew-in interfacing for filling pieces C • 60 × 30cm (24 × 12in) of dark blue starred fabric for the background (B, C, D) • 34 × 12cm (13½ × 5in) of fabric for the yellow borders • 40 × 18cm (15¾ × 7in) of fabric for the gold-patterned dark blue borders • 38 × 37cm (15 × 14½in) of wadding (batting) • 41 × 40cm (16¼ × 15¾in) of dark blue fabric for the backing

down over the heart by section 2. Turn your work over and sew the strip along the stitching line of section 2. Turn your work over again and trim the seam allowance short. Open out the strip of fabric, press it flat and pin it on to the broken stitching line.

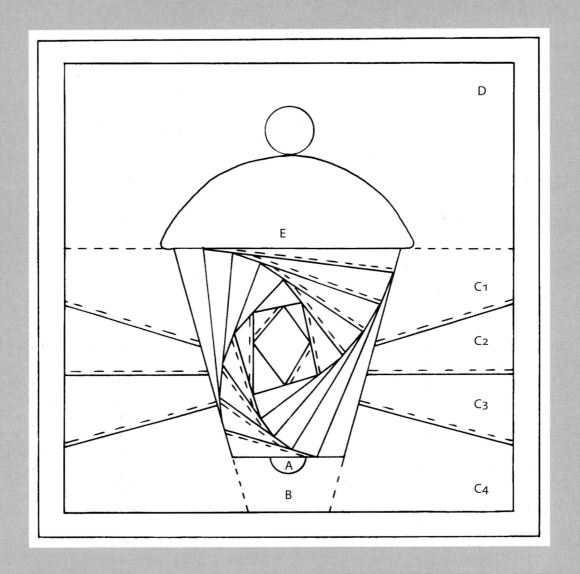

D

E

C1

C2

C3

A

B

C4

Lantern template and stitching guide

Enlarge by 236%

Copy and colour in the template using the colours of your fabrics. Use this template as a guide to cutting and stitching the background sections.

4 For the rest of section 2, take a strip of beige fabric measuring 5 × 4cm (2 × 1½in) and pin it right side up over the heart, keeping the upper edge level with the edge of the light yellow fabric. Turn your work over and stitch the strip along the broken line of section 2. Turn your work over again and trim the seam allowance short. Open out the strip of fabric, press it flat and pin it on to the next stitching line.

5 For section 3, take a strip of yellow-patterned fabric measuring 5 × 4cm (2 × 1½in) and pin it right side down over the heart by section 3. Turn your work over and stitch the strip along the stitching line of section 3. Turn your work over again and trim the seam allowance short. Open out the strip of fabric, press it flat and pin it on to the next stitching line.

6 For section 4, first take an intermediate strip of light yellow fabric measuring 5 × 2cm (2 × ¾in) and pin it right side down over the heart by section 4. Turn your work over and sew the strip along the stitching line of section 4. Turn your

work over again. Open out the strip of fabric, press it flat and pin it in place.

7 For the rest of section 4, take a strip of starred white fabric measuring 5 × 4cm (2 × 1½in) and pin it right side down over the heart, keeping the upper edge level with the edge of the light yellow fabric. Turn your work over and stitch the strip along the dotted line of section 4. Turn your work over again and trim the seam allowance short. Open out the strip of fabric, press it flat and pin it in place.

What to do next

Repeat the procedure described above from step 2 onwards, measuring out a generous strip length for each section you are going to cover. Follow the numbering and keep alternating the colours in the same order: dark yellow, light yellow and beige, patterned yellow, light yellow and starred white. Once section 24 is covered, tack the last strips to interfacing all

round just outside the outermost stitching line. Cut the lantern into shape, leaving a 6mm (¼in) seam allowance all round.

Putting it all together

1 Fold the small piece of beige-motif fabric, right sides together and trace on the semicircle A, allowing a small seam allowance all round. Stitch around the curved edge, trim the seam allowance and turn out. From dark blue starred fabric cut out section B (see page 90), adding a seam allowance all round. Stitch A and B to the bottom of the lantern in one go and then stitch A over B.

2 Trace the C filling pieces on the right of the design on to 20 × 14cm (8 × 5½in) of interfacing. This will form the left-hand side when the pieces of fabric are applied to the back. The narrow light yellow strips are fitted in between in the same way as on the lantern.

3 Turning the interfacing over, cover C1 with 8 × 11cm (3¼ × 4⅜in) of starred dark blue fabric and pin this in place. Lay a narrow strip of light yellow fabric right side down over the starred dark blue fabric by the edge of C2 and pin into place. Turn your work over and sew the pieces together along the broken line of C1. Turn your work over again and trim the seam allowance short. Open out the narrow light yellow strip, press it flat and pin it in place. Cut 7 × 11cm (2¾ × 4⅜in) of starred dark blue fabric into shape for C2. Lay this right side down over C1 and sew the pieces together along the continuous stitching line. Turn your work over yet again and trim the seam allowance short.

4 Now again sew a narrow strip of light yellow fabric along the broken line, and then 7 × 12cm (2¾ × 4¾in) of starred

dark blue fabric along the stitching line to form C3. To finish, sew a narrow light yellow strip to the last remaining broken line and 9 × 13cm (3½ × 5in) of starred dark blue fabric to the continuous stitching line to form C4. Tack the pieces of fabric to the interfacing along the outer edge just outside the stitching lines, and cut the C pieces into shape, adding a 6mm (¼in) seam allowance around the edges.

5 For the C pieces on the right-hand side of the lantern, trace the left-hand C pieces on to interfacing and fill as described above. Stitch both sets of C filling pieces on to the lantern. Stitch 14 × 30cm (5½ × 12in) of dark blue starred fabric on to the upper side (D).

6 For the lantern lid, fold 14 × 18cm (5½ × 7in) of beige-motif fabric, right sides together, to measure 7 × 18cm (2¾ × 7in). Trace the curve of E on the fold and stitch it tight. Trim the seam allowance short. Make a horizontal cut in the back and turn the lid right sides out through it. Stitch the lid at the top of the lantern.

Finishing off

Cut the fabric for the yellow borders into four strips measuring 34 × 3cm (13½ × 1¼in). Stitch the borders on to the top, bottom and sides. Cut the fabric for the gold-patterned dark blue borders into four strips measuring 40 × 4.5cm (15¾ × 1¾in) and stitch them on in the same way. Lay the quilt top and backing together right sides together, stitch them tight on three sides and part of the fourth side. Stitch the wadding to the back of the lantern and turn your work right sides out. Close the gap in the fourth side. Tack the layers together and quilt them as desired. Sew the ring on at the top with nylon thread.

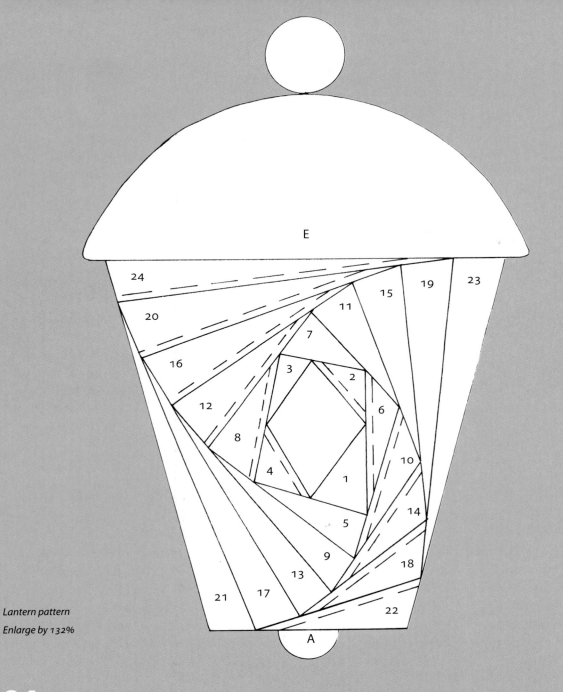

Lantern pattern
Enlarge by 132%

Acknowledgements

My thanks go to:

Herma, Tiny, Rieny, Harmke, Truus and Corrie of Quilt & Queck in Ugchelen
for their splendid pieces of handiwork and their enthusiasm;

Roelie Verhoek in Apeldoorn for her enjoyable and valuable course in
'Revolving log cabins';

Coby and Branco of Rouwendal Sewing machine Centre in Apeldoorn for
their lucid introduction to meandering and their good advice;

HUIS No.56, home decorators, in Ugchelen for the use of their delightful
shop as a setting for photographs of my iris quilts;

My home front for putting up with pins, pieces of fabric, etc. strewn around
the house, my tales about such incomprehensible matters as interfacing
and meandering, my refrain 'I haven't got time just now', my sighs and
groans at the computer and my frequent, sudden and alarming yells!